THE COLLECTED WORKS
OF HERMAN DOOYEWEERD

Series B, Volume 16

GENERAL EDITOR: D.F.M. Strauss

In the Twilight of Western Thought

*Studies in the Pretended Autonomy
of Philosophical Thought*

Series B, Volume 16

Herman Dooyeweerd

Paideia Press
2012

Library of Congress Cataloging-in-Publication Data

Dooyeweerd, H. (Herman), 1894-1977.
    [Lecture Series in the US. English 1960 / Edited 1999]
    In the Twilight of Western Thought / Herman
    Dooyeweerd
    p. cm

    Includes bibliographical references, glossary, and index
    ISBN 979-0-88815-217-6

    1. Philosophy. 2. Christian Philosophy. 3. Historicism.
    4. Philosophy and Theology. 5. Anthropology I. Title.

    This is Series B, Volume 16 in the continuing series
    The Collected Works of Herman Dooyeweerd
    (Initially published by Mellen Press, now published
    by Paideia Press)

    ISBN 979-0-88815-217-6

The Collected Works comprise a Series A, a Series B, and a Series C
    (*Series A* contains multi-volume works by Dooyeweerd,
    Series B contains smaller works and collections of essays,
    Series C contains reflections on Dooyeweerd's philosophy
    designated as: *Dooyeweerd's Living Legacy*, and
    Series D contains thematic selections from Series A and B)

A CIP catalog record for this book is available from the British Library.

The Dooyeweerd Centre for Christian Philosophy
Redeemer College Ancaster, Ontario
CANADA L9K 1J4

©PAIDEIA PRESS 2012
Grand Rapids, MI 49507

Printed in the United States of America

In the Twilight of Western Thought

Edited by
James K.A Smith
Villanova University, Villanova, Pa, U.S.A

Based upon a lecture series given by Dooyeweerd in North America during the late nineteen-fifties, this work was prepared in English by Dooyeweerd himself and first appeared in 1960, published by The Presbyterian and Reformed Publishing Company, Philadelphia, Pensylvania. It was reprinted in 1968 by The Craig Press, Nutley, New Jersey. Both of these earlier editions contained an Introduction by R J. Rushdoony. It has been incorporated also in this new edition and can be found on pages 137-142.

At the same time, this latest edition contains some significant new features. For instance, the text has been divided into four main parts and, with the exception of chapter eight, all other chapter headings have been revised or added by the editor. They are intended to more accurately indicate the development of the argument and to break up the text into more manageable sections, particularly for use in te-aching. The editor has also organized the running text by subdividing it into sections (§), some of which are further subdivided.

In order to further improve readability, certain other minor changes have been introduced in this edition, particularly with regard to spelling and grammar. Some originated with the editor while others were added by the general editor. All were made quite selectively and only with the intent of enhancing readability and understanding without in any way compromising the original text. In view of these changes and to facilitate comparison where deemed advisable, the pagination numbers of the original 1960 publication (and the 1968 reprint) have been incorporated in this revised edition and can be found between square brackets within the running text.

Additionally, it should be noted that the original edition provided no references. In this edition, all footnotes are the work of the editor. One of the primary purposes of these notes is the provision of references pertaining to the thinkers and themes Dooyeweerd engages in this book.

A more detailed description of the approach used by the editor in undertaking the editorial revision of this work together with his acknowledgments appears on pages 133-135.

Note : The editor's contribution to this volume was made possible in part by a fellowship grant from the Social Sciences and Humanities Research Council of Canada, whose support is gratefully acknowledged.

Contents

PART ONE

The Pretended Autonomy of Philosophical Thought

Chapter One

Chapter Five

Chapter Six

Chapter Seven

Chapter Eight

ADDENDA

Editor's Introduction

Dooyeweerd's Critique of 'Pure' Reason

James K.A. Smith

§ 1. The Project of *In the Twilight of Western Thought*

Originally delivered as lectures in various venues throughout North America,[1] Herman Dooyeweerd's In the Twilight of Western Thought was designed to be an introduction for English readers[2] to a philosophical movement which had its origins in the Reformational tradition in the Netherlands. Having made its way across the Atlantic under daunting epithets such as "De Wijsbegeerte der Wetsidee" and the "Philosophy of the Cosmonomic Idea," Dooyeweerd's vision of a radically Christian philosophy was initially confined – in North America – to a rather narrow group of Dutch-born and Dutch-educated philosophers and theologians working within the Reformed tradition. In the Twilight of Western Thought was intended to make this philosophy more accessible, serving as an introduction to his formidable systematic work, A New Critique of Theoretical Thought.[3] From his own pen, then, Dooyeweerd offers an introduction and résumé of his project.

---

1   The Reformed Fellowship funded a lecture tour in 1959, during which Dooyeweerd travelled throughout the United States and Canada. In the Twilight of Western Thought is based on this lecture series.

2   A similar introduction for French readers was provided in the pages of a French Reformed Journal, La Revue Réformée. See Herman Dooyeweerd, "Philosophie et théologie," La Revue Réformée 9 (1958), pp. 48-60; Idem., "La prétendue autonomie de la pensée philosophique;" "La base religieuse de la philosophie grecque;" "La base religieuse de la philosophie scolastique;" "La base religieuse de la philosophie humaniste;" "La nouvelle tâche d'une philosophie chrétienne," La Revue Réformée 10 (1959), pp. 1-76.

3   Herman Dooyeweerd, A New Critique of Theoretical Thought, 4 Vols., trans. David H. Freeman, H. de Jongste, and William S. Young (Amsterdam: H.J. Paris; Philadelphia: Presbyterian & Reformed Publishing Co., 1953-1955); The Collected Works, Series A, Vols. 1-4, The Edwin Mellen Press, Lewiston, N.Y., 1997.

a) The pretended autonomy of philosophical thought

What exactly is this project? The key to this question is found in the subtitle to the book; Dooyeweerd is here offering Studies in the Pretended Autonomy of Philosophical Thought. Both the genius and heart of Dooyeweerd's work lies in this 'critique' of reason – a delimitation of reason's claim to autonomy.[1] Thus, the beginning chapters of the book are also the most crucial: while philosophy from Plato to Husserl has claimed that reason operates apart from extra-philosophical 'commitments,' Dooyeweerd is intent on demonstrating that all theoretical thought – philosophy included – is ultimately grounded in both pretheoretical and supra-theoretical commitments which function as the condition of the possibility for theory. These commitments or beliefs are of an ultimate nature: they cannot be demonstrated, but are rather the basis for demonstration.[2] Thus we might describe Dooyeweerd's project as a certain 'critique of pure reason;' however, in contrast to Kant, Dooyeweerd's critique seeks to demonstrate that 'pure,' unalloyed reason is a myth, a pretended autonomy.

In chapter two, following the lead of Augustine and Calvin, Dooyeweerd points to these 'structural' commitments as an indication of the "innate religious impulse of the ego." Because of this "religious impulsion," the self finds its meaning in relation to an absolute – either the Origin of the self (the Creator), or in relation to a contrived or posited 'absolute' whereby the ego "absolutizes" an aspect of the temporal order as a substitute for its true origin.[3] Thus the religious impulse – which is structural, 'built-in' to the self – can take different directions: either a biblical direction in relation to the true Origin, or an apostate direction.

Also in chapter two, Dooyeweerd provides something of a catalogue of dominant apostate religious basic motives: the Greek form-matter motive, the scholastic nature-grace motive, and the humanistic nature-freedom motive. What is common to all of these apostate or non-biblical motives is their dialectical character: because they attempt to synthesize contradictory religious impulses or commitments, they experience an in-

1 As will be discussed below (in my §3 of this Introduction), Dooyeweerd's delimitation of reason's claim both draws upon and anticipates the concerns of postmodernism as it has developed from Heidegger and Derrida. As explained in my notes accompanying chapter one, 'critique' must be understood in the Kantian sense of marking the boundaries and limits of theoretical thought.

2 For a more extensive introduction to this project, the reader is encouraged to consult Roy A. Clouser, The Myth of Religious Neutrality: An Essay on the Hidden Role of Religious Belief in Theories (Notre Dame, IN: University of Notre Dame Press, 1991).

3 Dooyeweerd, again following Augustine and Calvin, will refer to this as 'idolatry,' but in a very technical sense (see § 6 of this Introduction).

ner tension which leads them into inescapable antinomies and dualisms. This stands in contrast to a radical biblical motive grounded in the theme of creation, fall into sin, and redemption by Jesus Christ. What is unique about the biblical basic motive is its integral character: it avoids all dualisms and uncovers the religious nature of the self, rather than positing a 'neutral' ego.

This unveiling of the religious root of the self is the basis for Dooyeweerd's critique: not unlike Heidegger's notion of Destruktion, Dooyeweerd's critique seeks to probe the depths of theoretical thought in order to uncover the fundamental commitments and faith which ground it. Once he has unveiled the pretended autonomy of theoretical thought as a myth, he has opened the way for a radical critique.[1] In turn, once these primordial commitments are unveiled and 'placed on the table,' as it were, then genuine philosophical dialogue becomes possible. Far from making interaction impossible, it is precisely this critique which makes communication possible.

b) Historicism and the sense of history

Having laid the foundation of a critique of theoretical thought in the first two chapters, the remaining chapters of the book simply explore the implications of this understanding of philosophy for various subjects and concerns. The first of these that Dooyeweerd engages, determined very much by intellectual currents in the first half of the twentieth century, is the question of historicism. The significance of historicism for Dooyeweerd's Christian philosophy is two-fold: first, it represents a challenge to the very notion of a 'supra-temporal' reality; second, it also represents one form of what Dooyeweerd would technically describe as 'idolatry.' As an absolutization of one of the modal aspects, namely that of the historical aspect, historicism has elevated history to the place of a transcendental condition; it has substituted something within creation for the Creator. Thus, the discussion of historicism is something of a 'case-study' in theoretical critique; today, one could provide a similar analysis of 'linguisticism' or 'biologism.' These chapters provide an example of the critique at work and provide clues for similar analyses which Dooyeweerd's critique both invites and demands.

c) Philosophy and Theology

As a philosophy which claims to be radically Christian whilst at the same time maintaining its autonomy with respect to theology, it was necessary for Dooyeweerd to delineate both the distinction and relation

---

1 One could also compare this to Gadamer's project of pointing out the presuppositions behind the Enlightenment's (purportedly neutral) prejudice against prejudice. See Hans-Georg Gadamer, Truth and Method, 2nd. rev. ed., trans. Joel Weinsheimer and Donald G. Marshall (New York: Continuum, 1993), pp. 270-277.

between philosophy and theology. And here we have another singular contribution to the historical discussion of this question.

Dooyeweerd's understanding of the relationship between theology and philosophy is first grounded in his earlier distinction between the theoretical attitude on the one hand and the natural, or pretheoretical attitude, as well as the level of supratheoretical commitments, on the other hand. All theoretical thought, as shown by Dooyeweerd in chapters one and two, is ultimately grounded in both pre- and supra-theoretical commitments. However, in the theoretical attitude, by means of abstraction, one 'steps back' to reflect upon a specific mode of reality. This 'stepping back' does not constitute a retreat to neutrality or objectivity; – one continues to operate on the basis of supratheoretical commitments. Rather, this process of abstraction requires the theoretical attitude to be relativized as unnatural, i.e. a revisable reflection upon pretheoretical experience.

Secondly, and based on this first distinction, Dooyeweerd emphasizes that theology, as a theoretical discipline, is distinct from the existential, supratheoretical commitments of Christian faith, which are commitments of the heart. Theology is a theoretical reflection upon this faith as it is manifested in the Scriptures and in the life of the Church. (Thus, for Dooyeweerd, theology is a branch of science which specializes in biblical research and interpretation and generally operates in and for the Church). This distinguishes it from religion which represents the supratheoretical commitment of the heart. With these distinctions in place, Dooyeweerd is able to point to a radically Christian philosophy that is not grounded in a particular theology but a philosophy that is nourished by the heart commitment to God as its radix or root. That commitment is not theoretical (i.e., theological) in nature but supratheoretical. Indeed, as Dooyeweerd suggests, even if one's heart is committed to God, one may nevertheless be working with a theology which is in fact rooted in a non-biblical religious commitment – such as he holds is the very problem inherent in what he describes as 'scholasticism' (chapter seven).

In these chapters, then, Dooyeweerd offers a unique understanding of the relationship between 'faith' and 'reason.' Unlike Aquinas, who posits that faith goes beyond natural, unaided reason, i.e. comes separately from or after it, Dooyeweerd points to the faith before reason, the commitments which ground reason in such a way that a 'natural, unaided' reason is impossible. What will pass for neutral rationality is in fact grounded in apostate religious commitments, such as the Greek form-matter motive. Dooyeweerd emphasizes that, in discussing the relationship between Jerusalem and Athens, we are not considering the relationship between religion and reason but rather the relationship between different religions. Athens, we must recall, had its temples, too.

The uniqueness of Dooyeweerd's understanding of this relationship is detected in his relationship to Augustine and the Augustinian tradition as unfolded in both the Franciscan tradition and Reformational thought, particularly that formulated by Calvin. As Dooyeweerd notes, while Augustine recognized the commitments of reason, he failed to distinguish between religion (as heart commitment) and theology (as theoretical reflection on faith); instead, Augustine collapsed the two and therefore conceived of theology as a 'Christian philosophy,' leaving no space for the separate development of a philosophy grounded in biblical faith. By carefully distinguishing religion and theology, Dooyeweerd opens a unique space for the development of an integral Christian philosophy which remains distinct from theology, that is, it must itself be nourished by and grounded in radically biblical faith.[1]

d) Towards a radically biblical anthropology

In response to existentialism, and developing themes deeply imbedded in his understanding of philosophy and the self, Dooyeweerd unveils his conception of the self as he perceives it from the biblical basic motive. Eradicating the dualisms and absolutizations that have plagued the history of philosophy – whereby the human person is reduced to the 'rational animal' – Dooyeweerd seeks to both honor the multidimensionality of the self, as well as the religious nature of the self which drives it to find meaning in its Origin.

Because of creational diversity, the human person experiences the world in a multiplicity of ways or modes: numerically, aesthetically, economically, ethically, etc. To 'define' the person by just one of these modes (generally the logical or rational in the history of philosophy) is to at the same time reduce the self to only one of its modes of experience and to absolutize one of the modal aspects. Rather, the multiplicity of modes in which we experience things must be honored. However, because of the innate religious impulse of the self (chapter two), the self also transcends itself – seeks meaning outside of itself in its Origin. This transcendent or "ek-static" character of the self points to the religious nature of the self as a self that seeks meaning in relation to an Absolute.

As Dooyeweerd sees it, existentialism proved to be an insufficient answer to just this question – the question of meaning. Because of the rise of historicism and the denial of the Absolute, existentialism sought to locate the meaning of the self in the temporal order, thereby absolutizing various aspects of experience. Thus Dooyeweerd develops his critique of existentialism against the horizon of the self's meaning which can only be found in its relation to its Origin – its Creator.

---

1   For a theology developed within this Dooyeweerdian framework, see Gordon Spykman, Reformational Theology (Grand Rapids: Eerdmans, 1992).

§ 2. A Genealogy of Dooyeweerd's Project in the Light of History

While Dooyeweerd makes a number of unique contributions, his project also builds on the history of philosophy and owes debts to a number of those within the tradition.[1] To recognize this is not to reduce his philosophy to this tradition; indeed, there are elements of his thought which cannot be located in the history of philosophy and Christian thought. Dooyeweerd's work becomes most interesting at precisely those points where he moves beyond his predecessors and strikes out in new territories. However, in order to see the trajectory of this thought, it will be helpful to note just a few important influences.

a) Augustine

As noted earlier, Dooyeweerd is not uncritical of Augustine; however, the doctor gratia is a fundamental ally in the arguments laid out in his project of In the Twilight. The Augustinian maxim, credum ut intelligam [I must believe in order to understand], points to the commitments of reason and functions as a precursor to the critique of the pretended autonomy of theoretical thought. In Augustine's account of knowledge, as well as in his vision of a Christian renewal of culture, Dooyeweerd finds an appreciation for the integral significance of faith for the development of a Christian philosophy.[2] Indeed, in his early Cassiciacum dialogues, we see the Christian Augustine undertaking his own 'reformation of the sciences,' seeking to both retrieve truth from his early studies but also to articulate a distinctly Christian understanding of self-knowledge. So also in De doctrina christiana, we see Augustine affirming the importance of research, but also noting the limits of such 'pagan' scholarship and the necessity for an explicitly Christian retrieval.

Dooyeweerd's project falls solidly within this Augustinian tradition of Christian scholarship, seeking to establish a Christian foundation for learning, envisioning a university of sciences grounded in Christian faith. Rather than confining faith's influence to theology alone, this Augustinian re-configuration of the faith/knowledge relationship opens the space for grounding the entire spectrum of the sciences in a radical faith.

Dooyeweerd and Augustine also share similar understandings of the 'transcendence' of the human self – that the person as created in the im-

---

1   For a general discussion of Dooyeweerd's intellectual debts, see Albert M. Wolters, "The Intellectual Milieu of Herman Dooyeweerd," in The Legacy of Herman Dooyeweerd, ed. C.T. McIntire (Lanham, MD: University Press of America, 1985), pp. 1-20.

2   It is important to note that Dooyeweerd does not hold Augustine to be 'scholastic' (that is, adopting an un-biblical starting-point), but rather views him as having a lack of precision regarding the distinction between a Christian philosophy and theology.

age of God can ultimately find meaning and rest only in its Maker (Confessions I.i.1). Because of this transcendence, or what Dooyeweerd describes as the 'concentric character of the self,' there is in the human person a drive to find meaning outside of itself. If that structural drive will not find its telos in the true Origin of the self, then it is directed to the world, where it experiences only dissolution and disintegration (Confessions II). It is not the 'world,' however, which is evil, but rather the self's relation to the world: if the self becomes absorbed in the world to the neglect and forgetfulness of the Creator, then it has 'fallen' into a mis-use of the world, enjoying what ought to be only used as that which points to the Origin. However, the self which finds its ultimate meaning or happiness in the Creator relates to the world in a different manner; thus the fundamental goodness of creation is maintained – yet another point of convergence and influence between Augustine and Dooyeweerd.

b) Calvin

As would be expected of a philosophy claiming to be 'Reformational,' Calvin is an important source for Dooyeweerd – precisely insofar as Calvin represents a retrieval and reappropriation of Augustinian Christianity. Thus, it is important to note that the Calvin who plays a role for Dooyeweerd is not a Calvinist; Dooyeweerd's retrieval leaps over the scholastic contamination of Calvin in the seventeenth and eighteenth centuries and thus brings to life a Calvin not concerned with the order of the decrees, but rather the reformer concerned only with "the knowledge of God and the knowledge of self" – an Augustinian, non-scholastic Calvin.[1]

c) Phenomenology

Perhaps most challenging for the new student of Dooyeweerd will be his distinctly European methodology and conceptual apparatus. Thus, it seems important to briefly note the role phenomenology plays in Dooyeweerd's project. While he is critical of phenomenology, Dooyeweerd nevertheless appropriates at least the language and concepts of phenomenology in order to unfold his critique. Most importantly, he makes a distinction between two attitudes: the theoretical attitude of reflection and the pretheoretical attitude of everyday life. The pretheoretical or 'naive' attitude (also described by Husserl as the 'natural' attitude) is the way in which we encounter the world in our everyday experience; we relate to concrete wholes: the tree, the desk, my car, my wife, etc. In the theoretical attitude, by means of a certain 'stepping--back' or abstraction, we reflect upon our pretheoretical experience. In

---

1   For this 'Calvin,' Dooyeweerd owed a debt to Dr. Abraham Kuyper's earlier retrieval. For Dooyeweerd's relation to Kuyper, see Wolters, op.cit., pp. 2-10.

this mode or attitude of reflection, we do not consider things as concrete wholes; rather, they are 'refracted' (as light through a prism) into a plurality of aspects. For instance, the book in my hand can be theoretically analyzed in a number of ways. It can be considered aethetically: the artwork on the cover, the fonts chosen in printing, etc. It can be considered sociologically: what role has the book played in society? How has it influenced various sectors? Why those sectors and not others? It could be considered as a work of literature, and so on. Everything, when analyzed theoretically, displays a multiplicity of aspects, each of which are the domain of a particular special science.

The naive/theoretical distinction plays an imporatnt role in phenomenological analysis; and it is important for the student to recall that these 'aspects' do not, properly speaking, exist. Or perhaps more specifically, they exist only in and for consciousness. Here again we see a Husserlian distinction between the Real and the Irreal. Trees, books, cars, and wives are real; but the economic, social, aesthetic, and numeric aspects are irreal, existing only in the attitude of abstraction, and only in and for consciousness. Thus, they are perceived only in the theoretical attitude: as I drive down the street, my car is not composed of these aspects, with, for example, the numeric under the hood and the social in the trunk. Instead, the aspects are different modes of experiencing the world, and it is this emphasis on experience which Dooyeweerd shares with phenomenology.

§ 3. The Significance of Dooyeweerd's Project in Light of Postmodernism

Why Dooyeweerd? Why Dooyeweerd now? In a sense, these are questions which will be answered only in reading Dooyeweerd. However, we can point to important shifts in contemporary philosophy which open a new space for the appreciation of Dooyeweerd's work and the significance of his project.

What is frequently (though perhaps not helpfully) described as 'postmodernism' is often considered to be a threat to Christian thinking but it does in fact open the way for just the kind of project Dooyeweerd envisages; indeed, we might even suggest that Dooyeweerd represents a proto-postmodern.[1] At the very least, postmodern critique also points to the commitments and presuppositions behind all that has traditionally trafficked under the banner of 'pure reason.' While also offering a challenge to Christian thought (one for which we perhaps should thank them), the work of Heidegger, Gadamer, Derrida, and Foucault have all, in one way or another, pointed to the faiths which ground philosophical discourse. As Alan Olson observes, "it may be that the deconstructive

---

1 Much as Malcolm Bull described Kuyper as being the first postmodern in "Who was the first to make a pact with the Devil?," London Review of Books (May 14, 1992), pp. 22-24.

mood of postmodernity is faith-inspired – even faith-obsessed in an ob-
scure sort of way."[1] By pointing to these same prior core commitments,
Dooyeweerd's project also sets about unmasking as a myth all that mas-
querades under the pretense of neutral and objective reason.

Within this environment, Dooyeweerd's work is significant both as an
early insight into this state of affairs, as well as an articulation of a distinctly Christian 'critique of pure reason.' As such, it also functions as
something of a manifesto: calling upon the community of Christian philosophers and theorists to engage in self-critique, and now seize the opportunity – in postmodernity – for the development of an integral Christian philosophy. As James Olthuis has suggested in a recent collection
of essays working within this tradition,

> "Understanding the primordial role of faith in theory formation,
> insisting that the pretended autonomy of theoretical thought is an
> illusion, witnessing to the reality of human brokenness, pursuing
> justice for all (not just for "us") in the public arenas of education,
> media, and politics – all have been compelling themes of the ref-
> ormational philosophical heritage for nearly a century. [...] These
> are perhaps a few indications of the sensitivities of this tradition
> to the concerns of postmodernism, and perhaps, we hope, reason
> to expect that our resources may be of some small help as we to-
> gether wrestle with the epochal shifts that shake and disturb us as
> we precipitously slide into a new millennium."[2]

Indeed, perhaps it is only now that we can begin to read Dooyeweerd.

---

1 Alan Olson, "Postmodernity and Faith," Journal of the American Academy of Religion 58 (1990), p. 37.

2 James H. Olthuis, "Love/Knowledge: Sojourning with Others, Meeting with Differences," in Knowing Other-wise: Philosophy at the Threshold of Spirituality, James
H. Olthuis, ed. (Bronx, NY: Fordham University Press, 1997), pp. 12-13. This entire
collection of essays represents the possibility of Dooyeweerd's significance for contemporary philosophical discourse and dialogue.

In the Twilight of Western Thought

PART ONE

The Pretended Autonomy of Philosophical Thought

Chapter One

A Critique of Theoretical Thought

§ 1. The necessity of a radical critique of theoretical thought

a) The contemporary crisis in philosophy

Every philosophy which claims a Christian starting-point is confronted with the traditional dogma[1] concerning the autonomy of philosophical thought, implying its independence of all religious presuppositions. It may be posited that this dogma is the only one that has survived the general decay of the earlier certitudes in philosophy. This decay was caused by the fundamental spiritual uprooting of Western thought since the two world wars. Nevertheless, it is the very crisis in the earlier fundamentals of philosophical thought which has paved the way for a radical criticism of the dogma of autonomy. Such a criticism is not only necessary from a Christian point of view, much rather it must be considered the primary condition of a truly critical[2] attitude of thought in every kind of philosophical reflection, irrespective of the difference in starting-point. For the acceptance of the autonomy of theoretical thought has been elevated to an intrinsic condition of true philosophy without its having been [2] justified by a critical inquiry into the inner structure of the theoretical attitude of thought itself.

---

1   The terms 'dogma' and 'dogmatic' have very precise meanings for Dooyeweerd. Dogmatic thought is, strictly speaking, 'uncritical.' However, this must be carefully distinguished from what Dooyeweerd describes as 'naive' thought. Dogmatic thought is uncritical thought within the theoretical attitude; naive thought belongs to the pre-reflective or pre-theoretical attitude.

2   Dooyeweerd's project of 'criticism' and 'critique' (especially as undertaken in his A New Critique of Theoretical Thought hereafter referred to as NC) must be understood in a Kantian and neo-Kantian sense, indicating not simply a negative 'destruction' of thought, but rather a delimiting of theoretical or philosophical thought, marking the boundaries of theory. For a discussion of this notion of critique, see Kant, Critique of Pure Reason, trans. Norman Kemp Smith (London: MacMillan, 1933), Prefaces to the First and Second Edition and B87-88.

So long as the belief in human theoretical reason as the ultimate judge in matters of truth and falsehood was unchallenged, this belief could be accepted as a theoretical axiom. But it is this very belief which, to a high degree, has been undermined in our day as a result of a radical historicism,[1] the influence of depth-psychology, the so-called Lebensphilosophie[2] and, at least in Europe, the powerful influence of Existentialism.[3] This makes the assertion of autonomy being the primary condition of philosophical thought all the more problematic, insofar as it is maintained in the present situation of Western philosophy.

b)   The structural necessity for a critique of theoretical
autonomy

But apart from the present crisis of all former certitudes, there are other reasons for making the dogma concerning the autonomy of philosophical thought into a critical problem. In the first place, this pretended autonomy, which is considered the common basis of ancient Greek, Thomistic-scholastic and modern secularized philosophy, lacks that unity of meaning necessary for such a common foundation. In Greek philosophy it had a meaning quite different from that in Thomistic scholasticism. In both of them it was conceived in a sense quite different from that which it assumed in modern secularized thought. As soon as we seek to penetrate to the root of these fundamentally different conceptions, we are confronted with a fundamental difference in presuppositions [3] which surpasses the boundaries of theoretical thought.

In the final analysis, these very presuppositions determine the meaning ascribed to this autonomy. This does not agree with the traditional dogmatic view of philosophical thought. For this view implies that the ultimate starting-point of philosophy should be found in this thought itself.[4] But due to the lack of a univocal sense, the pretended autonomy cannot guarantee a common basis for the different philosophical trends. On the contrary, it appears that again and again this dogma has impeded a real contact between philosophical schools and trends that prove to differ in their deepest, supra-theoretical[5] presuppositions. This is the

---

1   For Dooyeweerd, Wilhelm Dilthey would be representative of this school. He engages this movement much more extensively in chapters 3 and 4 below.

2   This would include phenomenology, and particularly the work of Edmund Husserl.

3   This would include Martin Heidegger (though perhaps wrongly so), and French philosophers and authors Jean-Paul Sartre and Albert Camus. Dooyeweerd engages existentialism more extensively in chapter eight below.

4   This is precisely Kant's claim: in his critique, Reason itself is called upon to be its own judge and "tribunal." See Critique of Pure Reason, Axi. Below, Dooyeweerd will describe this as "immanence" philosophy since it seeks the criteria for critique within theoretical thought itself.

5   Dooyeweerd distinguishes three different 'attitudes' or modes of thinking: (1) a pre-theoretical attitude which is also described as "naive" or (following Husserl), the

second reason why we can no longer accept it as an axiom which is not problematic but simply gives expression to an intrinsic condition of true philosophy. For if all philosophical currents that pretend to choose their starting-point in theoretical reason alone, had indeed no deeper presuppositions, it should be possible to settle every philosophical argument between them in a purely theoretical way. But the factual situation is quite different. A debate between philosophical trends, which are fundamentally opposed to each other, usually results in a reasoning at cross-purposes, because they are not able to find a way to penetrate to each other's true starting-points. The latter seem to be masked by the dogma concerning the autonomy of philosophical thought. And as long as there exists a fundamental difference in the [4] philosophical views of meaning and experience, it does not help if, in line with contemporary logical positivism,[1] we seek to establish criteria for meaningful and meaningless philosophical propositions and require their verifiability.

It may be granted that this factual situation does not yet prove the impossibility of an autonomous philosophical theory which lacks any presupposition of a supra-rational character. But it is, in any case, sufficient to show that it is necessary to make the dogmatical assertions concerning the autonomy of theoretical thought into a *critical problem.* This problem should be posed as a quaestio iuris. This means that in the last analysis we are not concerned with the question as to whether philosophical thought in its factual development has displayed an autonomous character making it independent of belief and religion. Much rather, the question at issue is whether this autonomy is required by the inner nature of thought, and thus is implied in this nature as an intrinsic possibility. This question can only be answered by a transcendental criticism of the theoretical attitude of thought as such. By this we understand a radically[2] critical inquiry into the universally valid conditions[3] which alone make theoretical thought possible, and which are required

"natural" attitude. This is the mode of everyday being-in-the world, experiencing objects and persons as concrete wholes. (2) In the theoretical attitude, one abstracts from and reflects upon pretheoretical experience, refracting it into a multiplicity of 'modes' or 'aspects' (this is discussed in much more detail below). Because this requires abstraction from everyday experience, theoretical thought is also, in a sense, 'unnatural.' (3) Dooyeweerd here discusses the supra-theoretical level, which exceeds the limits of theoretical thought and is the realm of faith commitments.

1   Dooyeweerd is thinking of the Austrian heirs of August Comte who are referred to as the Vienna Circle. Subsequent 'analytic' philosophers such as A.J. Ayer would also be included here.

2   'Radical' is used in a very precise sense: derived from the Latin radix, it refers to a critique which penetrates to the 'roots,' to the foundational presuppositions which underlie theoretical thought. This requires a 'radical reading,' a reading deeply, beneath the surface.

3   For Kant also, critique demarcates the conditions of possibility of thought and experience, viz. space and time (Critique of Pure Reason, Transcendental Aesthetic). Again, Dooyeweerd's project bears analogies to Kant, but also radical differences.

by the inner structure and nature of this thought itself.

c) *Transcendental versus transcendent critique*

This latter restriction shows the fundamental difference between a transcendent and a transcendental critique of philosophical thought. A transcendent critique has nothing to do with the inner structure [5] of the theoretical attitude of philosophical thinking and its necessary conditions. Much rather, it criticizes the results of a philosophical reflection from a viewpoint which lies beyond the philosophical point of view. A theologian, for instance, may criticize the Kantian view of autonomous morality from the viewpoint of the Christian faith. But this critique remains dogmatic and worthless from the philosophical viewpoint so long as the inner point of connection between Christian faith and philosophy remains in the dark and the autonomy of philosophical thought is granted as an axiom. Theology itself is in need of a transcendental critique of theoretical thought, since it is bound to the theoretical attitude and always has philosophical presuppositions.[1]

Philosophy, on the other hand, is also in need of this criticism since it is the only way for it to conquer a theoretical dogmatism which lacks a radical self-critique. Under the influence of the dogmatical acceptance of the autonomy of philosophical thought such a radical critique was excluded up to now. Neither Kant, the founder of the so-called critical transcendental philosophy, nor Edmund Husserl, the founder of modern phenomenology, who called his phenomenological philosophy 'the most radical critique of knowledge,'[2] have made the theoretical attitude of thought into a critical problem. Both of them started from the autonomy of theoretical thinking as an axiom which needs no further justification. This is the dogmatical presupposition of their theoretical inquiry which makes the critical character of the latter problematic and masks their real starting-point, which, as a matter [6] of fact, rules their manner of positing the philosophical problems.

We do not insist that the adherents of this dogma abandon it from the outset. We only ask them to abstain from the dogmatical assertion that it is a necessary condition of any true philosophy and to subject this assertion to the test of a transcendental critique of theoretical thought itself.

---

1   This critique is taken up below in Part Three, "Philosophy and Theology," chapters 5-7.

2   Cp. Edmund Husserl, Ideas Pertaining to a Pure Phenomenology and to a Phenomenological Philosophy, First Book: General Introduction to a Pure Phenomenology, trans. F. Kersten (The Hague: Martinus Nijhoff, 1983), pp. 141-149.

6

§ 2   Analysis of the Theoretical Attitude

a)   Modal aspects of our experience of reality

How is the theoretical attitude of thought characterized?[1] What is its inner structure by which it differs from the non-theoretical attitude of thinking? It displays an antithetic structure wherein the logical aspect of our thought is opposed to the non-logical aspects of our temporal experience. To comprehend this antithetical relation it is necessary to consider that our theoretical thought is bound to the temporal horizon of human experience and moves within this horizon. Within the temporal order, this experience displays a great diversity of fundamental aspects, or modalities[2] which in the first place are aspects of time itself. These aspects do not, as such, refer to a concrete what, i. e., to concrete things or events, but only to the how, i.e., the particular and fundamental mode, or manner, in which we experience them. Therefore we speak of the modal aspects of this experience to underline that they are only the fundamental modes of the latter. They should not be identified with the concrete phenomena of empirical reality, which function, in principle, in all of these aspects. Which, then, are these fundamental modes of our experience? I shall enumerate them briefly.[3]

Our temporal empirical horizon has a numerical aspect, a spatial aspect, an aspect of extensive movement, an aspect of energy in which we experience the physico-chemical relations of empirical reality, a biotic aspect, or that of organic life, an aspect of feeling and sensation, a logical aspect, i. e., the analytical manner of distinction in our temporal experience which lies at the foundation of all our concepts and logical judgments. Then there is a historical aspect in which we experience the cultural manner of development of our societal life. This is followed by

---

1   For important and helpful discussions of Dooyeweerd's 'theory of theory,' see Hendrik Hart, "Dooyeweerd's Gegenstand Theory of Theory," in The Legacy of Herman Dooyeweerd, ed. C.T. McIntire (Lanham, MD: University Press of America, 1985), pp. 143-166; and D.F.M. Strauss, "An Analysis of the Structure of Analysis," Philosophia Reformata 49 (1984), pp. 35-56.

2   What Dooyeweerd describes as 'aspects,' 'modes,' 'modalities,' or 'modal spheres,' are simply aspects of a concrete thing which become distilled only in the theoretical attitude. It is important to understand that these 'modes' do not exist; that is, in Husserl's terminology, they are Irreal, existing only in theoretical consciousness. For instance, this desk is a concrete whole; but when I consider it in the theoretical attitude, I recognize that it has an aesthetic aspect (its design), an economic aspect (its price and its place in a market as a commodity), etc. Dooyeweerd's most extensive discussion of 'modal theory' is found in A New Critique of Theoretical Thought, Volume II: The General Theory of Modal Spheres.

3   There has been some discussion in subsequent Dooyeweerd scholarship regarding the enumeration of the spheres. See Calvin Seerveld, "Dooyeweerd's Legacy for Aesthetics: Modal Law Theory," in The Legacy of Herman Dooyeweerd, pp. 62-68. See also NC 1:3.

the aspect of symbolical signification, lying at the foundation of all empirical linguistic phenomena. Furthermore there is the aspect of social intercourse, with its rules of courtesy, politeness, good breeding, fashion, and so forth. This experiential mode is followed by the economic, aesthetic, juridical and moral aspects, and, finally, by the aspect of faith or belief.

b) The diversity of modal aspects within time

This whole diversity of modal aspects of our experience makes sense only within the order of time.[1] It refers to a supra-temporal, central unity and fulness of meaning in our experiential world, which is refracted in the order of time into a rich diversity of modi, or modalities of meaning, just as sunlight is refracted by a prism in a rich diversity of colors. A simple reflection may make this clear. In the order of time, human existence and experience display a great diversity of modal aspects, but this diversity is related to the central unity of the human selfhood, which, as such, surpasses all modal diversity of our temporal experience. In the order of time the divine [8] law for creation displays a great diversity of modalities. But this whole modal diversity of laws is related to the central unity of the divine law, namely, the commandment to love God and our neighbor.

Within the theoretical attitude of thought we oppose the logical aspect of our thinking and experience to the non-logical modalities in order to acquire an analytical insight into the latter. These non-logical aspects, however, offer resistance to our attempt to group them in a logical concept and this resistance gives rise to theoretical problems. Such theoretical problems are, for example, What is the modal meaning of number? of space? of organic life? of history? of economy? of law? of faith? And these problems are of a philosophical character, since they refer to the fundamental modi of human experience, which lie at the foundation of all our concrete experience of diversity in things, events, and so forth.

It is true that in principle the different modal aspects delimit also the special viewpoints under which the different branches of empirical science examine the empirical world. This merely corroborates our view concerning the modal diversity of our experiential horizon and our view

---

1   On Dooyeweerd's notion of time, see Hendrik Hart, "Problems of Time: An Essay," in The Idea of a Christian Philosophy (Toronto: Wedge, 1973), pp. 30-42. J. Stellingwerff has noted the impact of Heidegger's work Sein und Zeit upon Dooyeweerd's concept of time. See J. Stellingwerff, "Elementen uit de ontstaansgeschiedenis der reformatorische wijsbegeerte," Philosophia Reformata 57 (1992), p. 188.

of theoretical thought in general. But these special sciences[1] do not direct their attention upon the inner nature and structure of these modal aspects as such, but rather upon the variable phenomena which function in them in a special manner. The inner nature and structure of the special modal aspects which delimit their field of research is a presupposition of every special science. [9] It is only philosophy which can make this presupposition into a theoretical problem. For it is impossible to conceive the special meaning and inner structure of a modal aspect without having a philosophical insight into the whole temporal coherence of all the different modal aspects of our temporal horizon of experience. The reason is that every aspect can reveal its proper modal meaning only in this total coherence which expresses itself in its own inner structure. This is the reason that this modal structure displays a great diversity of components, or moments, which in turn reveal the modal meaning of the aspect concerned only in their total coherence.

In the first place, every aspect, or mode of experience, has a modal kernel which guarantees its irreducible special meaning. But this modal kernel of its meaning can only express itself in a series of so-called analogical moments[2] referring to the modal kernels of all the other aspects of our experience which precede or succeed, respectively, the aspect concerned in the temporal order. In accordance with the different direction of their reference, they may be distinguished into retrospective and anticipatory moments. Viewed in themselves these analogical moments are multivocal since they occur also in the other experiential aspects wherein they display a different meaning. Their proper modal sense is only determined by the modal kernel of the aspect in whose structure they function. Nevertheless, they maintain their coherence with the aspects to which they refer.

Let us take, for example, the sensitive aspect of our [10] experience. Its modal kernel is that irreducible moment of feeling which cannot be defined in a logical way. "Was man nicht definieren kann, das sicht man als ein Fòhler an."[3] But this German adage is applicable to the modal kernel of each aspect. The nuclear moment of feeling, however, unfolds its modal sense only in an unbreakable coherence with a whole series of analogical moments, referring backward to earlier arranged aspects of our experience. Feeling has its own mode of life, bound to the aspect of

---

1 The corresponding German term would be positive Wissenschaften; it is important to understand 'science' indicating theoretical inquiry in a broad sense, not just the natural or 'hard' sciences. What North Americans refer to as the 'humanities' are understood on the continent as Geisteswissenschaften, human sciences.

2 Each aspect has a 'core' meaning; however, it cannot be discovered or understood apart from its interrelationship will other aspects of the concrete whole. See below §§ 13-14.

3 'What one cannot define, one sees as with an antenna [or 'feeler'].'

organic life by its sensory moment. It is emotional, and emotion is a sensitive and intensive mode of movement, referring backward to the modal kernel of the original aspect of extensive movement. It has its own mode of energy or force, with grades of intensity, its causes and effects, by which it manifests its coherence with the physico-chemical aspect. It manifests its coherence with the spatial aspect in spatial analogies, namely, the subjective sensation of spatiality and the objective sensory space of our sensory perception, whose modal meaning is quite different from that of pure mathematical space, physical space, biotic space, and so forth.

All these structural moments of the sensitive aspect are also present in more developed animal feeling. But in the human experience this aspect unfolds also structural moments of an anticipatory character in which its coherence with the subsequently arranged aspects of our temporal horizon manifests itself. Feeling for logical coherence, cultural feeling, linguistic feeling, aesthetic feeling, legal feeling, moral feeling, [11] and so forth, are such anticipatory analogical moments in the modal structure of the sensitive aspect which deepen and open up, or disclose, its modal meaning. Thus this modal structure reflects the whole coherence of the different aspects of our experience in a special modal sense. And the same holds true with respect to each other aspect, as I have shown in detail in the second volume of my work: A New Critique of Theoretical Thought.[1] This may be called the universality of each experiential aspect within its own modal sphere.

§ 3. A transcendental critique of theoretical thought

As I mentioned, the theoretical problem concerning these modal structures of our experience is of a philosophical character. But a transcendental critique of philosophical thought is concerned with previous problems which are of a still more fundamental character. The antithetical structure of the theoretical attitude of thought gives rise to the question: Does this antithetical relation between the logical aspect and the non-logical aspects of our temporal experience correspond with the internal structure of the latter? The answer must be negative.

This theoretical antithesis originates only in our intention to conceive the non-logical aspects of our experience by means of an analytical dissociation whereby they are set apart. In this way we oppose them to the logical aspect of our thought and to each other in order to conceive them in a logical concept. But this analytical dissociation of the aspects pre-

---

1   General Theory of Modal Spheres.

supposes their theoretical abstraction from the continuous [12] bond of their coherence in the order of time. That is to say, we cannot get them in the grip of a logical concept without separating them from all the other aspects in an abstract logical discontinuity. But this does not mean a real[1] elimination of their continuous bond of coherence, which, on the contrary, remains the necessary condition and presupposition of their theoretical dissociation and opposition. It merely proves the impossibility of conceiving the continuity of this coherence in an analytical way by theoretical thought.

a) First problem: the coherence of diverse modal aspects (theoretical antithesis)

Thus the first basic problem of our transcendental critique of theoretical thought may be more precisely formulated as follows: What is the continuous bond of coherence between the logical aspect and the non-logical aspects of our experience from which these aspects are abstracted in the theoretical attitude? And, how is the mutual relation between these aspects to be conceived?

By raising this problem we exclude in principle the false dogmatical idea that theoretical thought would be able to penetrate to empirical reality as it really is, or even to a metaphysical realm of being, which would be independent of possible human experience.[2] The false presupposition that the theoretical separation of the logical aspect from all the other aspects of our experience corresponds to true reality, has led to very singular metaphysical conclusions. The Greek philosopher, Aristotle, concluded from this presupposition that the theoretical-logical function of thought has an activity quite independent of the [13] organic life of the body and the sense-organs. From this he derived his thesis that the active intellect is immortal in contrast to the individual man.[3] He knew very well that the several concepts of theoretical thought are of an abstract character; but he did not realize that the separation of the logical function of thought itself from all the other aspects of our temporal experience is only a result of theoretical abstraction and can accordingly not agree with integral reality. The dogma concerning the autonomy of theoretical thought impeded the insight into its real structure.

---

1 That is, opposed to 'abstract' or what Husserl describes as Irreal.

2 Dooyeweerd is not affirming the traditional Kantian doctrine of the 'thing-in-itself' (Ding-an-sich) or noumenon to which we are denied access; rather, his critique is closer to Heidegger's hermeneutic phenomenology, which affirms that we only have access to the world as it is given to us, who are conditioned by presuppositions. In NC, Dooyeweerd explains that the "structural horizon of human experience" (the 'world') is interpreted by a "subjective a priori complex" (2:548); thus, he continues, "We only gain access to [this structural horizon] in a subjective-theoretical way" (2:554).

3 Aristotle, De Anima, III.5 (430a10-25).

This was also the reason why the fundamental difference between the theoretical and the non-theoretical attitude of thought was lost sight of, or was at least entirely misinterpreted. The non-theoretical attitude is that of the so-called naive experience, or of common sense experience. It lacks entirely that antithetical relation between the logical and the non-logical experiential modes which is characteristic of the theoretical attitude of thought and experience. Here our logical function remains completely immersed in the continuity of the temporal coherence between the different aspects. Our attention is neither directed upon abstract special aspects of concrete phenomena, as in special scientific research, nor upon the inner nature and structure of the aspects as such, as in the philosophical theory concerning the fundamental modes of experience. Much rather we here experience concrete things and events in the typical structures of individual totalities which in principle [14] function in all the modal aspects of our temporal horizon in their continuous mutual coherence. Our logical mode of distinction is entirely embedded in this integral experience. Our pre-theoretical logical concepts are only related to things and events as individual wholes, and not to the abstract modal aspects of their empirical reality. These aspects are only experienced implicitly in the things and events themselves, and not explicitly in their analytical dissociation and opposition to the logical function of thought.

Before we were able to abstract the numerical relations from concrete numerable things, we learned to count by means of an abacus or bead-frame by shifting the little red and white balls. All of us, in the naive attitude of experience, connect the spatial form of a circle to the representation of something round such as a hoop or wheel. All of us also connect the physico-chemical relations to concrete substances such as water, salt, and so forth; by no means do we have an abstract theoretical notion of energy relations as such. In the naive attitude of experience things are always conceived in the integral coherence of their modal aspects.

How is this integral character of naive experience possible? How is it to be explained that even inanimate things and natural events such as a thunderstorm function in all the modal aspects of our naive experience in their continuous temporal bond of coherence? This is possible only by means of the subject-object relation[1] which is inherent in this experiential attitude. [15] In this relation we ascribe to things and events objective functions in such aspects, in which they can never function as subjects. As adults, who have outgrown infantile animistic representations, we know very well that water is not a living substance. Nevertheless, in the biotic aspect of our experience we ascribe to it the objective function of being a necessary means for life. We ascribe to it objective

---

1 For more extensive discussion, see NC, 2:366-413.

sensory qualities and some objective logical characteristics, objective functions in our socio-cultural life, and so forth. Notwithstanding the fact that in this subject-object relation water functions in all the modal aspects of our experience, we are aware of the fact that it belongs to the kingdom of inorganic matter, which is qualified by physico-chemical qualities.

A bird's nest, on the contrary, is typically qualified by its subject-object relation to the organic and sensory life of the bird, although we also ascribe to it objective functions in the post-biotic and post-sensory aspects of our experiential horizon. In naive experience we conceive it as an individual whole, qualified by this subject-object relation to the bird's life; and this finds expression in the name whereby the thing is symbolically signified. The nest itself has an objective function in the aspect of symbolical signification. A plastic work of fine art is experienced as an individual whole, functioning in all the modal aspects of our temporal horizon, but typically qualified by its aesthetic subject-object relation.[1] It expresses the aesthetic vision of the artist objectively in the material of his formation. A cathedral can only be experienced [16] as an architectural whole, typically qualified by its objective destination, which finds expression in its entire inner structure, namely, that it has been destined for the use of the ecclesiastical cult. This means that its qualifying subject-object relation is only to be found in the modal aspect of faith, though it functions equally in all the other aspects of experience.

We cannot, at this time, engage in a more detailed inquiry into the typical total structures of individuality, which the things and events display in naive experience.[2] In the present context we are interested only in the general significance of the subject-object relations which guarantee the integral character of this non-theoretical experience. By means of these relations the latter embraces in principle all the modal aspects of a thing or event in their continuous bond of coherence within the structural framework of an individual whole and without any analytical dissociation of these different aspects.

It is entirely foreign to naive experience to ascribe object functions to things or events apart from the possible subject functions to which they are related. The sensory color red is ascribed to a rose only in relation to every possible normal human sensory perception under adequate light conditions, not as an occult quality of a metaphysical substance which would exist in itself beyond any relation to possible sensory perception. This metaphysical conception is meaningless if the color red is under-

---

1   It should be noted that Dooyeweerd's theory of modal spheres opens the space for aesthetics as a special science. For further discussion, see NC, 3:109-127, and Calvin Seerveld, "Dooyeweerd's Legacy for Aesthetics: Modal Law Theory," Op. cit.

2   For further discussion, see NC, Volume III, Part I.

stood as an objective sensory quality of the flower. If it is meant in the [17] sense of the modern physical theory of light refraction, it is also meaningless since this theory does not relate to metaphysical substances, but to the energy-aspect of empirical phenomena.

The subject-object relations of naive experience are, consequently, fundamentally different from the antithetical relations which characterize the theoretical attitude of thought. Subject and object are certainly distinguished in the non-theoretical attitude, but they are never opposed to each other. Rather, they are conceived in an unbreakable coherence. In other words, naive experience leaves the integral structural coherence of our experiential horizon intact. The theoretical attitude of thought and experience breaks it asunder by an analytical dissociation of its modal aspects.

It is no wonder that modern philosophical theories of knowledge which hold to the dogma of the autonomy of theoretical thought were incapable of doing justice to naive experience. Losing sight of the fundamental difference between the pre-theoretical subject-object relations inherent in naive experience and the antithetical relation characteristic of the theoretical attitude, they interpreted naive experience itself as an uncritical theory. This theory was called the theory of naive realism, or the copy-theory. According to this theory, naive experience was supposed to assume that our sensory perception gives us an adequate image of things as they are 'in themselves' – as metaphysical substances, apart from human experience. A refutation of this theory with the aid of the experimental [18] results of scientific research on the one hand and epistemological arguments on the other, was supposed to be a refutation of naive experience itself. A strange misunderstanding, indeed! Naive experience is not at all a theory which may be refuted by scientific and epistemological arguments. It does not identify empirical reality with its abstract sensory aspect and it lacks the metaphysical notion of an objective world of things in themselves beyond the world of experience. Naive experience is much rather a pre-theoretical datum, corresponding with the integral structure of our experiential horizon in its temporal order. Any philosophical theory of human experience which cannot account for this datum in a satisfactory way must be erroneous in its fundamentals.

b) Second problem: the relation between theoretical and naive experience (theoretical synthesis)

After this confrontation of the theoretical and the pretheoretical attitudes of thought and experience, we may continue our critical inquiry into the former. We have seen that the theoretical opposition of the logical function of thought to all the non-logical aspects of experience gives rise to the theoretical problem: How can we acquire a logical concept of these non-logical experiential modes? But theoretical philosophical thought cannot stop at this theoretical problem; it must proceed from the theoretical antithesis to a theoretical synthesis, or union, between the logical and the non-logical aspects if a logical concept of the non-logical modes of experience is to be possible. When we reflect on this requirement, we are confronted [19] with a new fundamental problem which may be formulated as follows: What is the central reference point in our consciousness from which this theoretical synthesis can start? This question touches the core of our inquiry. By raising this second basic problem, we subject every possible starting-point of theoretical thought to our transcendental criticism.

Now it is evident that the true starting-point of a theoretical synthesis, or union, between the logical and the non-logical experiential modes, howsoever it may be chosen, is by no means to be found in one of the terms of the antithetical relation. It must necessarily transcend the theoretical antithesis and relate the aspects that were dissociated and opposed to one another to a central unity in our consciousness. For one thing is certain: the antithetical relation, with which the theoretical attitude of thought stands or falls, offers in itself no bridge between the logical aspect and the non-logical experiential modes opposed to it. And in the temporal order which guarantees their unbreakable coherence we do not find a central reference point transcending the diversity of the modal aspects.

This means that the dogma concerning the autonomy of theoretical thought must lead its adherents into a seemingly inescapable impasse. To maintain this autonomy they are obliged to seek their starting-point in theoretical thought itself. But by virtue of its antithetic structure, this thought is bound to the inter-modal theoretical synthesis between the logical [20] and the non-logical aspects. Even a so-called formal logic cannot do without a synthesis between the logical aspect and that of symbolical signification, which are by no means identical.

Now there are as many modalities of theoretical synthesis as there are experiential modes of a non-logical character. There is a synthetical thought of mathematical, physico-chemical, biological, psychological, historical and linguistic nature as well as others of like character. In which of these possible special theoretical viewpoints may philosophical thought find the starting-point of its theoretical and synthetical total view of our experiential horizon? No matter how the choice is made, it invariably amounts to the absolutization[1] of a synthetically conceived special modal aspect.

This absolutization is the source of all isms in the theoretical view of human experience and empirical reality. They result from the attempt to reduce all other modal aspects of our temporal horizon of experience to

---

1   The notion of 'absolutization' is developed more fully below in chapter 2, § 6.

simple modalities of the absolutized aspect. Now, such isms as mathematicism, biologism, sensualism, historicism, and so forth, are uncritical in a double respect. Firstly, they may never be justified from a purely theoretical standpoint. On the contrary, theoretical thought, because of its antithetical and synthetical character, is bound to the irreducible diversity of the fundamental modes of experience and their interrelations. In the whole sphere of theoretical thought there is nowhere room for the absoluteness of an aspect. The absolutization as such can, therefore, not originate in theoretical thought itself. It [21] testifies much rather to the influence of supra-theoretical motives which are obscured by the pretended autonomy of philosophical thought.

Secondly, in every absolutization of a special synthetical viewpoint the fundamental problem concerning the starting-point of the theoretical synthesis returns unsolved. For this synthesis cannot nullify the irreducible diversity between the logical aspect and the non-logical experiential mode, which in the theoretical antithesis, is made into its theoretical problem. Any attempt at reducing the logical term of the theoretical antithesis to the non-logical, or vice versa, is tantamount to a dogmatic elimination of the problem.

But is the above argument sufficient to demonstrate that philosophical thought, by virtue of its inner structure, cannot find its starting-point in itself? We should not draw this conclusion too hastily. Kant, the father of the so-called critical transcendental philosophy, was of the opinion that he could show a starting-point in theoretical thought itself, which is the central reference point of every special scientific synthesis and the condition of its possibility. Can the autonomy of theoretical thought be demonstrated by way of Kant's so-called critical transcendental method? Let us consider his argument.

To discover the immanent starting-point of theoretical thought as the central reference point of theoretical synthesis, Kant points to the necessity of a critical self-reflection in our theoretical acts of thinking by directing our reflection toward the thinking I. [22] This hint contains, indeed, a great promise. For it is beyond doubt that as long as theoretical thought in its logical function continues to be directed merely to the opposed modal aspects of our experiential horizon, it remains dispersed in the theoretical diversity of these aspects. Only when theoretical thought is directed toward the thinking ego can it acquire the concentric direction towards an ultimate unity of our consciousness to which the whole modal diversity of our experiential horizon must be related.[1] If you ask all the special sciences engaged in anthropological research: "What is man?" you will receive a great diversity of information referring to the different aspects of temporal human existence. These answers are

---

1 The 'concentric' or ekstatic character of self is the theme of chapter 2 below.

doubtless, important. But even by combining all these different special viewpoints from which they are given, you cannot find an answer to the central question: "Who is man himself in the central unity of his self-hood?" The path of critical self-reflection is, consequently, the only one that can lead to the discovery of the true starting-point of philosophical thought.

c)   Third problem: the origin of the ego

But here a new fundamental problem arises, which may be formulated as follows: "How is the concentric direction of theoretical thought to-wards the ego possible, and what is its source?" It is beyond doubt that this problem, too, is of a truly transcendental nature. For by virtue of its dissociative character theoretical thought is bound to an antithetic basic relation, which as such can only lead it in a divergent direction. Conse-quently, the concentric direction of theoretical thought upon the human selfhood cannot [23] originate from theoretical reason itself. Neverthe-less, self-reflection is necessary in a transcendental critique to reveal the real starting-point of philosophical thinking. Kant did not raise the prob-lem mentioned since he held to the dogma of the autonomy of theoreti-cal thought. Therefore he was obliged to seek the central reference point of the theoretical synthesis in the logical aspect of thought, which he calls understanding.

The notion, "I think," so he says, must necessarily accompany all my representations if they are to be altogether my representations. But this "I think" is according to him only that subjective logical pole of thought which can never become the object of my thinking since it is the logical center from which every act of thinking must start. Kant calls this sup-posed logical center of theoretical thought the "transcendental logical unity of apperception,"[1] or also the transcendental logical subject, or "ego." He assumes that it is a subjective logical unity of an absolutely simple character, so that it is indeed a central unity without a single multiplicity or diversity of components. This transcendental-logical I is, according to Kant, to be distinguished sharply from the empirical ego, the psycho-physical human person, which we can perceive in time and space. It does not belong to empirical reality. It is much rather the gen-eral condition of any possible act of thought; and as such it has no indi-viduality of any kind. It is the theoretical-logical subject to which all [24] empirical reality can be opposed as its object counter-pole, its ob-ject of knowledge and experience.

Kant emphasizes that from this transcendental logical notion, "I think," not an iota of self-knowledge is to be gained, since our knowl-edge is restricted to the sensorily perceptible phenomena in time and

1   Kant, Critique of Pure Reason, A107/B132.

space, which are the very object of the logical I. But has Kant succeeded in showing a real starting-point of the theoretical synthesis within the logical aspect of thought itself? The answer must be negative. We have seen that the reference point of the theoretical synthesis cannot be found within the theoretical antithesis between the logical aspect and the non-logical aspects of experience, which are made into the problem of ana-lytical inquiry. But Kant's transcendental-logical subject is exactly con-ceived of as the subjective-logical pole of this antithesis. As such it can never be the central reference point of our experience in the temporal order with its diversity of modal aspects.

The "cogito" from which Kant starts cannot be a merely logical unity. It implies the fundamental relation between the ego and its acts of thought, which can by no means be identical. A logical unity, on the other hand, can never be an absolute unity without multiplicity. This contradicts the modal nature of the logical aspect. Thus Kant's view of the transcendental ego lands in pure mythology. It implies an intrinsi-cally contradictory identification of the central I with its subjective logi-cal function.

To maintain the dogma of the autonomy of theoretical thought, Kant has allowed the real starting-point [25] of his critique of theoretical rea-son to remain in the dark. It is the task of our radical critique to uncover it.

The third transcendental problem which we have raised, namely, "How is the concentric direction of theoretical thought upon the ego possible, and whence does it originate?" cannot be solved without knowing the inner nature of the human I, i. e., without self-knowledge. Since the days of Socrates, philosophy has sought for this self-knowledge. But the human I as the center of human experience and existence displays an enigmatic[1] character. As soon as I try to grasp the I in a philosophical concept it recedes as a phantom and dissolves itself into nothingness. It cannot be determined by any modal aspect of our experience, since it is the central reference point to which all fundamen-tal modes of our temporal experience are related. A logical I does not exist, neither a psycho-physical I, nor a historical, nor a moral I. All such philosophical determinations of the ego disregard its central char-acter.

David Hume was quite right when, from his sensualistic viewpoint, he dissolved the concept of the selfhood into a natural relation between

---

1   As will be seen in chapter 2, Dooyeweerd's understanding of the self falls within the Augustinian tradition which affirms that knowledge of self and God are inextricably linked. And thus, to not know God is to not know oneself, to experience the anxiety of self-alienation. For Augustine's account of the enigmatic character of the self, see his Confessions, Books VII and X.

our successive sensations.[1] The Socratic requirement: "Know yourself," leads philosophical reflection to the limits of all theoretical thought. Must the philosopher stop at these limits in order to save the dogma of the autonomy of theoretical reason? But this would be pure self-deceit, since without a radical critical self-reflection we ignore the inescapable transcendental [26] problems implied in the intrinsic nature of the theoretical attitudes of philosophical thought itself. The uncritical absolutization to which the ignoring of these problems has led makes it necessary to overcome also this last bulwark of theoretical dogmatism. This can be done by directing our theoretical thought to its central supra-theoretical reference point, the human I, or selfhood.

It is not theoretical thought that can give itself this concentric direction. It is the central ego which alone can do so, from a supra-theoretical starting-point. What is the inner nature of this enigmatical I? And how can we arrive at real self-knowledge? These central questions will be the subject-matter of our second lecture [chapter two] on the general subject of the pretended autonomy of reason.

---

1 See David Hume, A Treatise of Human Nature, Second Edition, ed. P.H. Nidditch (Oxford: Oxford University Press, 1978), p. 207: "what we call a mind, is nothing but a heap or collection of different perceptions."

Chapter Two

The Concentric Character of the Self

§ 4. The enigmatic character of the self

As we saw in my first lecture, consideration of the concentric direction of our theoretical thought upon the human ego appeared to be necessary in order to discover the real starting-point of philosophical reflection. This consideration, however, gave rise to a new problem, which we formulated as follows: How is this concentric direction possible and what is its real origin? This problem had not as yet found a solution, but it fixed our attention upon the enigmatical character of this I. The latter turned out to be the central reference point of our entire temporal horizon of experience with its diversity of modal aspects. As such it turned out to be also the real center of every theoretical act of thinking, and, consequently, to be a necessary presupposition of philosophical thought in all of its manifestations.

But, as we saw earlier, each attempt to grasp this ego in a logical concept, and to define it with the aid of synthetically conceived modal aspects of our experiential horizon, appeared to be doomed to failure. If the state of disorientation resulting from such attempts remains limited each time to a strictly transitional phase and does not turn into a widespread phenomenon that finds expression in some new aggressively persistent world- and life-view, it may soon be overcome. But when it turns out to have a deeper cause than the breakdown of belief in the tradition and to be, in fact, the result of a process whereby the ultimate spiritual foundations of a whole civilization are being increasingly undermined, we may rightly speak of a fundamental crisis in that civilization.

The mystery of the central human ego is that it is nothing in itself, i.e., viewed apart from the central relations wherein alone it presents itself. But the first of these relations, namely, that of the selfhood to the temporal horizon of our experience, cannot determine the inner character of the ego, except in a negative sense. The central unity of the selfhood is not to be found in the modal diversity of the temporal order. A physico-psychical I does not exist, neither a logical, a historical, nor a moral self.

§ 5.   The self's relation to others: intersubjectivity

However, let us turn to the other central relations wherein our ego functions, in order to consider whether they can determine the inner nature of our ego in a positive sense. Contemporary personalistic and phenomenalistic philosophy has laid all the stress upon the interpersonal I-thou relation, which is essential to self-knowledge. The Jewish thinker, Martin Buber,[1] sharply contrasts this inter-personal relation to the subject-object relation of our experience. In his opinion, the former reveals itself in a real spiritual meeting of the persons concerned, whilst the latter, in contrast, gives expression only to a ruler's[2] [29] attitude, inherent in experience, which objectifies the world in order to control it. Disregarding Buber's view of experience, which apparently is oriented to the Humanist science ideal in its natural scientific sense, we must posit that, in any case, experience and the inter-personal relation cannot be contrasted to one another. For experience itself implies an inter-personal relationship between one ego and another. This relation belongs to the central sphere of our experiential horizon and eliminating it amounts to annihilating self-consciousness. My selfhood is nothing without that of yours, and that of our fellow-men. In other words, there exists a central communal relation between the individual centers of experience, lying at the foundation also of any temporal communal relation in theoretical thought.

But can this central I-thou relation give a positive content to our self-consciousness? Can it lead us to a solution of the riddle of the human ego? So long as it is viewed only in itself, this relation is no more able to do so than the relation of our ego to the temporal horizon of our experience. The reason is that the ego of our fellow-men confronts us with the same mystery as our own selfhood. The Swiss psychiatrist and philosopher, Binswanger,[3] strongly influenced by contemporary existentialism and personalism, says that the communal relation of you-I is qualified as an inter-personal meeting in love. But what is meant by this

---

1   Martin Buber, I and Thou, trans. Ronald Gregor Smith, Rev. Ed. (Edinburgh: T. & T. Clark, 1958).

2   For most post-Cartesian philosophy, the relation between subject and object is one of domination, control over nature, and over other persons; the self (ego) is conceived as a 'master' or 'ruler.' While Buber rejects this model for interpersonal relations, he retains the motif of domination in the ego's relation to things which are 'objectified' by thought. As will be seen below, Dooyeweerd's thought is distinctly anti-Cartesian in this regard.

3   Ludwig Binswanger (b. 1881), Swiss psychiatrist and important founder of existential psychiatry, influenced by Heidegger (initiated during Heidegger's brief stay at the Haus Baden sanatorium in Badenweiler in 1946). For a representative work, see Ludwig Binswanger, Being-in-the-World, trans. Jacob Needleman (New York, 1963).

meeting in love? Within the temporal horizon of our experience the love-relation displays a great diversity of modal meaning and typical societal [30] structures.[1] There is a difference in principle between the sexual eros, or affection, as an instinctive sexual drive, and the moral love of the neighbor. Both, in turn, differ in principle from the theoretical Platonic love of beauty, truth and goodness. The love between husband and wife, or that between parents and their children, is of a different typical societal character from the love between a venerated master and his disciples, or from our inter-personal relations to our compatriots, implied in the common love of country. But none of these temporal love-relations can be of that central nature which is essential to the human selfhood.

It may be that there exists a central love-relation which is capable of determining the inner meaning of my ego in its essential communal relation to that of my fellowmen. But as long as this love-relation is only viewed as a temporal relation between me and my fellowmen, we must posit that we do not know what is really meant by it. And as long as terms such as interpersonal meeting and love are used in philosophical anthropology in an undefined sense, a suspicion of mystification is bound to arise.

§ 6. The religious relation to the Origin of the self

Thus, both the central relations, which we have considered up to this point, are empty in themselves, just like the human ego that functions in them. But there is a third central relation which points above the human selfhood to its divine Origin. This is the central religious relation between the human ego and God, in whose image man was created. It may be objected that this relation exceeds the boundaries [31] of philosophical thought. This is certainly true, since philosophical thought is bound to the temporal horizon of experience with its modal diversity of aspects. Nevertheless, it can only be this religious relation from which philosophical thought in its theoretical attitude can acquire the concentric direction upon our selfhood. For it is beyond doubt that theoretical thought, viewed apart from the central ego, cannot give itself this central direction. It is only the thinking I that is capable of critical self-reflection.

But if our philosophical thought is not directed upon that central religious relation, which points above the thinking ego to its absolute Origin, all critical self-reflection is doomed to result in the conclusion that the ego is nothing. This conclusion, however, is meaningless, since it

---

1   For Dooyeweerd, love is the "modal meaning-kernel" or "modal meaning-nucleus" of the ethical aspect (NC 2:154-163).

would imply the negation of theoretical thought itself; for the latter is nothing without the ego. Thus a philosophical self-reflection which is not directed upon the central religious relation will be obliged to seek the ego within the temporal horizon of our experience in order to avoid this nihilistic result. Thereby it abandons the critical attitude and devises an idol of the central ego by absolutizing one of the modal aspects of our temporal consciousness. This is the origin of such idols as the psychological, the transcendental-logical, the historical and the moral ego.[1]

a) The structural religious tendency of the self

However, we have established that such absolutizations are not to be explained on the basis of theoretical thought itself. They rather betray the influence of a supra-theoretical central motive, which can only [32] be of a religious character. For it is only in its central religious relation to its divine origin that the thinking ego can direct itself and the modal diversity of its temporal world upon the absolute. The inner tendency to do so is an innate religious impulsion of the ego.[2] For, as the concentration point of all meaning, which it finds dispersed in the modal diversity of its temporal horizon of experience, the human ego points above itself to the Origin of all meaning, whose absoluteness reflects itself in the human ego as the central seat of the image of God. This ego, which is empty in itself, is only determined in a positive sense by its concentric relation to its divine origin. And it is also from this central relation that the relation of our ego to its temporal horizon and its central communal relation to the ego of our fellow-man can take a positive content.

1　Since the ego is nothing in itself but only in relation to its Origin, and since theoretical thought requires the affirmation of a self or ego, then the ego – if it is to avoid the complete dissipation of the self and theoretical thought – must either find its meaning in relation to its Origin (God), or it will be forced to 'absolutize' one aspect of the temporal sphere, treating it as though it were absolute. This is why Dooyeweerd describes this 'absolutization' as 'idolatry,' where one of the temporal, modal aspects is substituted for the true, transcendent Origin. This is very similar to Augustine's understanding of idolatry in De Vera Religione, x.18-xv.29.

2　The historical antecedent for this notion of an 'innate religious impulsion' is found in Calvin's sensus divinitatis: "There is within the human mind, and indeed by natural instinct, an awareness of divinity [sensus divinitatis]" (Institutes I.iii.1). It is important to note, particularly in relation to Dooyeweerd, that this is not a 'natural' knowledge of (the true) God as in Aquinas; it is not a sensus Dei but a sensus divinitatis. Rather than saying that humans possess a natural, 'built-in' knowledge of the true God, Calvin and Dooyeweerd are saying that human beings are, in their very essence, religious beings. Thus, for both Calvin and Dooyeweerd, even idolatry is evidence of this "seed of religion" (Institutes I.iii.1) which drives humanity to create gods. Dooyeweerd describes this 'drive' as an "innate religious impulsion of the ego." This religious impulsion is part of the structure of humanity, but because of the Fall, it may take an apostate direction (see below).

The innate religious impulsion of the ego in which its central relation to its divine Origin finds expression, takes its content from a religious basic motive as the central spiritual motive power of our thinking and acting.[1] If this basic motif is of an apostate character it will turn the ego away from its true Origin and direct its religious impulse upon our temporal horizon of experience, to seek within the latter both itself and its Origin. This will give rise to idols originating from the absolutization of what has only a relative meaning.[2] But even in this apostate manifestation, the religious character of the selfhood as the point of concentration of human nature continues to reveal itself.[3] Even in its absolutizing of the [33] relative, the thinking and acting ego transcends its temporal horizon. It is subjected to a central law that we may call the religious concentration law of our consciousness, by which it is obliged to transcend itself in order to find the positive meaning of itself.

b)   The religious basic motive

Therefore, the real starting-point of philosophical thought cannot be the ego in itself, which is an empty notion. It can only be the religious basic motive, operative in the ego as the center of our temporal horizon of experience. This alone gives the ego its positive dynamic character also in its central interpersonal relation to the other egos and to its divine origin. In other words, such a basic motive implies the only three central relations in which the ego can manifest itself.

As soon as philosophical thought begins to lose its definite direction in consequence of the undermining of its religious basic motive, it falls into a state of spiritual decadence and becomes a victim to a radical relativism and nihilism. At present the symptoms of such a spiritual uprooting can readily be established in what is called the fundamental crisis of contemporary Western thought. In this crisis the distress and disintegration of the human ego itself is revealed. For the ego necessarily dissolves itself into nothingness when it loses its direction towards the Absolute.

The religious basic motive is always of a central communal character and gives expression to a common spirit which unites those who are

---

1   The religious 'impulsion', which is structural, takes it definite or contentful direction from the religious 'basic motive.' That is, as below, the impulsion may take an apostate direction, turning away from the true origin.

2   Idols are the product of the absolutization (that is, the attribution of absoluteness, not confined to temporal horizon) to something that is relative, bound to the temporal horizon (that is, one of the modal aspects taken to direct/constitute the whole).

3   That is, the structure continues to be manifest even in a false direction. Dooyeweerd is not suggesting that everybody believes in God, but rather that everybody is committed to some god; that is, everyone is religious, a believer in something. Here he is a more faithful reader of Calvin than contemporary 'Reformed epistemologists.'

ruled by it. It rules a thinker even when, in consequence of the traditional [34] dogma concerning the autonomy of philosophical thought, he is not aware of its true nature. As a communal motive it lies at the foundation of a community of thought, insofar as it guarantees an ultimate possibility of mutual understanding even between philosophical trends which vehemently combat one another.

Within the temporal order of our experiential horizon, to which our philosophical thought is bound, the influence of the religious basic motive upon philosophy is bound to two conditions. First, it must give rise to a common belief within the faith-aspect[1] of our experience; secondly, it must gain a socio-cultural power within the historical aspect[2] of human society, so that it has become a formative factor in human culture. The faith-power, which it develops in its temporal manifestation, makes it into the leading principle of our thought. The socio-cultural power, which it has acquired in the process of history, guarantees the temporal foundation of its social influences. The faith-aspect of its manifestation within the temporal horizon of experience can be made into the theoretical object of a theological investigation. The historico-cultural aspect of its influence can be made into the theoretical object of historical research. But the religious basic motive itself in its central sense can no more become the object of a theoretical inquiry than the central ego itself.[3]

In our transcendental critique, this religious basic motive is only to be approached in the concentric direction of our theoretical thought on the thinking [35] ego. But this thinking ego is then to be taken in its positive sense as the religious center of our temporal experience, which, as such, transcends the bounds of philosophical thought, but is nevertheless its necessary presupposition.

If the religious basic motives did not manifest their central influence within the inner development of philosophical thought itself, philosophy

1 The 'faith-aspect' (also described as the 'pistic' or 'certitudinal' aspect) must be distinguished from the religious basic motive. For further discussion, see James H. Olthuis, "Dooyeweerd on Religion and Faith," in The Legacy of Herman Dooyeweerd, pp. 23-29.

2 That is, the religious basic motive is 'manifested' or 'expressed' in historical manifestations.

3 While Dooyeweerd affirms that the religious basic or ground motive cannot be the object of theoretical research, below (§ 7) he nevertheless attempts to disclose and analyze four basic religious motives. Thus, on this point we find a certain tension in Dooyeweerd's thought. For a discussion, see Jacob Klapwijk, "Epilogue: The Idea of a Transformational Philosophy," in Jacob Klapwijk, Sander Griffioen and Gerben Groenewoud, eds., Bringing Into Captivity Every Thought: Capita Selecta in the History of Christian Evaluations of Non-Christian Philosophy (Lanham, MD: University Press of America, 1991), pp. 241-266.

would have nothing to do with them. But it is the very task of a radical transcendental critique to show this influence in order to break through any form of theoretical dogmatism which masks its true starting-point by the deceptive axiom of the autonomy of theoretical reason. And our previous inquiry into the inner structure of the theoretical attitude of thought, and the formulation of the three transcendental basic problems to which this attitude gives rise, have uncovered the necessary inner point of connection between the theoretical sphere of our philosophical reflection and the central supratheoretical sphere of our consciousness, which is of a religious character.

The development of Western philosophy has been chiefly ruled by four religious basic motives, which have acquired a socio-cultural power in the history of Western civilization. The first is the Greek form-matter motive, whose religious meaning I shall explain presently. The second is the radical biblical basic motive of creation, fall into sin, and redemption by Jesus Christ in the communion of the Holy Spirit; the third is the scholastic motive of nature and [36] grace; the fourth is the modern Humanistic motive of nature and freedom.

c) The dialectical character of non-biblical ground motives

Before engaging in a brief explanation of these four basic motives, and of their central influence upon philosophical thought, I will make some remarks concerning the general character of the non-biblical ones. In contrast to the central motive of the Holy Scriptures, they present a dialectical character. This means that they are intrinsically divided by an irrevocable religious antithesis, caused by the fact that they are composed of two central motive powers, which are in polar opposition to one another. They involve every philosophical thought that finds itself in their grip, in a dialectical process, wherein this thought is alternately driven towards the one or the other pole of its religious starting-point. What is the origin of this intrinsic conflict in the dialectical basic motives? As to the scholastic motive of nature and grace, it originates from the attempt at a mutual accommodation of the biblical and the Greek or Humanistic basic motives, which exclude one another in principles. As to the Greek and the Humanistic motives, their inner conflict originates in the fact that they divert the innate religious impulse of the human ego from its true origin and direct it upon the temporal horizon of experience with its diversity of modal aspects. By seeking itself and its absolute origin in one of these aspects, the thinking I turns to the absolutization of the relative.

Now I have shown in the preceding lecture on this same subject that the modal sense of every experiential [37] aspect can only reveal itself in an unbreakable correlation with that of all the others. This means that the religious absolutization of particular aspects cannot fail to call forth their correlates, which in the religious consciousness begin to claim an absoluteness opposite to that of the deified ones. In other words, any idol that has been created by the absolutization of a modal aspect evokes its counter idol. Consequently, the dialectical basic motives are always characterized by an ultimate antithesis. This antithesis divides the religious impulse of the ego and thereby prevents the insight into the radical unity of the human selfhood in its central relation to the whole of our temporal horizon of experience.

Further, it is impossible to solve this antithesis by means of a genuine synthesis. The reason is that this antithesis urges itself upon the human consciousness with the mythical semblance of being absolute and it does so with an inner necessity because of its religious character. This is the fundamental difference between a theoretical and a religious dialectic. The former is inherent in the antithetical relation which characterizes the theoretical attitude of thought. It requires a theoretical synthesis between the logical aspect of our thought and the non-logical experiential aspects which we have set in opposition to it and which constitute its field of research. And this synthesis has turned out to require a starting-point in the central religious sphere of our consciousness. But when this central [38] starting-point itself presents an antithesis between two opposed motive powers, there is no other central starting-point to be found to solve this antithesis by means of an ultimate synthesis. The religious antithesis does not allow any real solution so long as the human ego finds itself in the grip of the dialectical basic motive that has called it into being. In this case there remains no other way out than to attribute the primacy to one of the opposed motives, which implies a religious depreciation, or at least, a subordination of the other. The periodic shifting of the primacy from the one motive to the other causes a dialectical process in philosophical thought that has its central starting-point in such a dialectical basic motive. This is why one and the same dualistic basic motive can give rise to polarly opposed philosophical tendencies, which at first sight seem to have nothing in common.

It is a regular phenomenon in the development of the religious dialectic in its expression within a philosophical course of thought that after or before a critical phase leading to a sharp separation of the two opposite motives, there arises a tendency to reconcile them by means of a so-called dialectical logic. Such an attempt testifies to the lack of a critical mind in philosophical reflection. Therefore, it is no wonder that the imaginary synthesis effected by means of such a dialectical logic dissolves itself again into a definite antithesis as soon as philosophy arrives at or returns to a critical attitude. We meet with all these traits of a dialectical process in the developments of Western philosophy [39] insofar as it has been ruled by the three dialectical basic motives mentioned.

This will appear in the second part of this lecture, in which we shall explain the influence of these motives upon Western thought.

§ 7. Outline of religious basic motives of western thought[1]

a) Greek form-matter motive

The central motive of Greek philosophy, which we have designated as the form-matter motive in line with the Aristotelian terminology, originated from the meeting of the pre-Homeric religion of life and death, with the younger, cultural religion of the Olympian gods. The older religion deified the ever-flowing stream of organic life, which issues from mother earth and cannot be bound to any individual form. In consequence, the deities of this religion are amorphous. It is from this shapeless stream of ever-flowing organic life that the generations of perishable beings originate periodically, whose existence, limited by a corporeal form, is subjected to the horrible fate of death, designated by the Greek terms anangkē or heimarmenē tuchē. This existence in a limiting form was considered an injustice since it is obliged to sustain itself at the cost of other beings so that the life of one is the death of another. Therefore all fixation of life in an individual figure is avenged by the merciless fate of death in the order of time. This is the meaning of the mysterious utterance of the ancient Greek philosopher, Anaximander, which reads "the (divine) Origin of all things is the apeiron"[2] (that is [40] to say, that which lacks a limiting form). "The things return to that from which they originate according to destiny. For they pay to each other penalty and retribution of their injustice in the order of time."[3]

The central motive of this religion, consequently, is that of the shapeless stream of life eternally flowing throughout the process of birth and decline of all that exists in a corporeal form. This is the original religious sense of the matter-principle in Greek philosophy. It issued from a deification of the biotic aspect of our temporal horizon of experience and has found its most suggestive expression in the ecstatic cult of Dionysus, imported from Thrace.

The form-motive, on the other hand, was the central motive of the younger Olympian religion, the religion of form, measure and harmony. It was rooted in the deification of the cultural aspect of classical Greek society. This motive found its most profound expression in the cult of the Delphian god, Apollo, the legislator. The Olympian gods have left mother earth with its ever-flowing stream of organic life and its inescap-

---

1 For similar analyses of religious ground motives, see NC Volume I, Part II; and Dooyeweerd, The Roots of Western Culture, Collected Works, Series B, Volume 3.

2 Anaximander, Fragments 103A-C, in The Presocratic Philosophers, eds. G.S. Kirk and J.E. Raven (Cambridge: Cambridge University Press, 1969), pp. 105-106.

3 Fragment 103A, in Ibid., p. 107.

able anangkē. They have acquired the Olympus as their residence and have a personal and immortal form, imperceptible to the eye of sense, an ideal form of a perfect and splendid beauty, the genuine prototype of the Platonic idea as the imperishable metaphysical form of true being. But these immortal gods have no power over the anangkē, the inexorable fate of death. Remember the utterance of Homer in his Odyssey: "The immortals too cannot [41] help lamentable man when the cruel anangkē strikes him down." This is why the younger Olympian religion was only accepted as the public religion of the Greek polis, the city-state. But in their private life the Greeks continued to hold to the old earthly gods of life and death.

The form-matter motive, originating in the religious consciousness of the Greeks from the meeting of these two antagonistic religions, was not in itself dependent upon the mythological and ritual form of the latter. As its central basic motive it ruled Greek thought from the very beginning. The autonomy claimed by Greek philosophical theories over against the popular belief implied merely an abandonment of those mythological forms of the latter which were bound to sensuous representation. It did not mean a break with the form-matter motive, as such. To the contrary it was much rather the common religious starting-point of all Greek thinkers. It was this very basic motive, which alone guaranteed a real community of thought between Greek philosophical tendencies, polarly opposed to one another. It determined the Greek view of nature, or physis, which excluded in principle the biblical idea of creation; it also ruled the classical Greek meaning of the terms eidos and eide, which are only understandable from the religious significance of the Greek form-motive. It lay at the foundation both of the Greek metaphysical view of being in its opposition to the visible world of becoming and decline, and of the Greek views of human nature and [42] human society. Because of its dialectical character, it has involved Greek thought in a dialectical process that displays all the traits which we have briefly indicated.

b) The radical biblical motive

The second basic motive of Western thought is the radical and central biblical theme of creation, fall into sin and redemption by Jesus Christ as the incarnate Word of God, in the communion of the Holy Spirit. This basic motive is the central spiritual motive power of every Christian thought worthy of this name. It should not be confused with the ecclesiastical articles of faith, which refer to this motive, and which can be made into the object of a dogmatic theological reflection in the theoretical attitude of thought. As the core of the divine Word-revelation,[1] it is

---

1   For Dooyeweerd, the "divine Word-revelation" is distinct from the particular revelation in Scripture. He discusses this further below in Part III, "Philosophy and Theology," where similarities to (and differences from) Karl Barth become manifest. For a discussion, see Olthuis, op. cit., p. 25.

independent of any human theology. Its radical sense can only be explained by the Holy Spirit, operating in the heart, or the religious center of our consciousness, within the communion of the invisible Catholic church.

This basic religious motive has uncovered the real root, or center, of human nature and unmasks the idols of the human ego, which arise by seeking this center within the temporal horizon of our experience with its modal diversity of aspects. It reveals the real positive meaning of the human ego as the religious concentration-point of our integral existence; as the [43] central seat of the imago Dei in the positive direction of the religious impulse of the ego upon its absolute Origin. Furthermore, it uncovers the origin of all absolutizations of the relative, namely, the negative, or apostate direction of the religious impulse of the human ego. Thereby it reveals the true character of all basic motives of human thought which divert the religious impulse towards the temporal horizon. This, then, is also the radical critical significance of the biblical basic motive for philosophy since it frees the thinking ego from the prejudices, which, because they originated from absolutizations, fundamentally impede a philosophical insight into the real and integral structure of the temporal order of experience. Therefore, this biblical basic motive is the only possible starting-point of a Christian philosophy in its genuine sense. But the development of such a philosophy has been prevented again and again by the powerful influence of Greek philosophy, and later on by the rise of the scholastic basic motive of nature and grace.

In the first phase of Christian thought, in which the Augustinian influence was predominant, the central working of this biblical basic motive was restricted to dogmatical theology. The latter was erroneously equated with Christian philosophy, which implied that philosophical questions were only treated within a theological context. Accordingly, the Augustinian rejection of the autonomy of philosophical thought over against the divine Word-revelation amounted to the denial of this autonomy over against dogmatical [44] theology, which was considered the queen of the sciences. This latter view was not biblical at all, but rather taken from the Aristotelian metaphysics, which had ascribed this royal position to a philosophical theology of which all other sciences would be the slaves.[1] In fact, the philosophical fundamentals of Augustine's

---

1   Aristotle, Metaphysics VI and XII. There is a historical problem with suggesting that Augustine's understanding of the relationship of the sciences came from Aristotle. It is not impossible, but unlikely. The same themes can be found in a Platonic and neo-Platonic philosophical theology.

thought were, in the main, taken from Hellenistic philosophy and only externally accommodated to the doctrine of the Church.

c) The scholastic nature-grace motive

In the second phase, beginning with the rise of Thomism, philosophy and dogmatical theology were sharply distinguished. But at the same time a third religious basic motive arose, which excluded the radical and integral influence of the central biblical motive on philosophy. This is the motive of nature and grace, which ever since has been the starting-point of scholastic philosophy as it developed both in Roman Catholic and Protestant[1] circles. It originally aimed at a mutual accommodation of the biblical and the Greek religious basic motives. But since the Renaissance it could also be serviceable to a mutual accommodation of the biblical and the modern Humanistic starting-points. It implied the distinction between a natural and a supra-natural sphere of thought and acting.

Within the natural sphere a relative autonomy was ascribed to human reason, which was supposed to be capable of discovering the natural truths by its own light. Within the supra-natural sphere of grace, on the contrary, human thought was considered to be dependent on the divine self-revelation.[2] Philosophy [45] was considered to belong to the natural sphere; dogmatical theology, on the other hand, to the supra-natural sphere. In consequence, there was no longer a question of Christian philosophy. Philosophical thought was, in fact, abandoned to the influence of the Greek and Humanist basic motives in their external accommodation to the doctrine of the Church. These motives were masked by the dogmatic acceptance of the autonomy of natural reason. The scholastic meaning ascribed to this autonomy was determined by the nature-grace theme. Natural reason should not contradict the supra-natural truths of the Church's doctrine, based on divine revelation. This implied an external accommodation of either the Greek or the Humanistic philosophical conceptions to this ecclesiastical doctrine as long as the ecclesiastical authority was factually respected by the students of philosophy. The Thomistic attempt at a synthesis of the opposite motives of nature and grace, and the ascription of the primacy to the latter found a clear ex-

---

1 On Protestant Scholasticism, see Richard A. Muller, Post-Reformation Reformed Dogmatics, Volumes 1 and 2 (Grand Rapids, MI: Baker, 1987, 1993).

2 Aquinas, Summa Theologiae, Ia. qu. 1, , and Expositio super librum Boethii De trinitate, qq. 1-2 (trans. Armand Maurer, Faith, Reason and Theology [Toronto: Pontifical Institute of Mediaeval Studies, 1987], pp. 13-55). As Aquinas emphasizes in In Boeth., his position marks a departure from Augustine's account of 'illumination' (In Boeth., qu. 1, art. 1).

pression in the adage: Gratia naturam non tollit, sed perficit (Grace does not cancel nature, but perfects it).[1]

But the dialectical character of the nature-grace motive clearly manifested itself in the late medieval nominalistic movement.[2] The Thomistic synthesis of nature and grace was replaced by a sharp antithesis. Any point of connection between the natural and super-natural sphere was denied. This was the beginning of shifting the primacy to the nature-motive. The process of secularization of philosophy had started. [46]

d) The humanistic nature-freedom motive

The fourth religious basic motive that acquired a central influence on western thought is that of modern Humanism, which arose and developed from the time of the Italian Renaissance of the 15th century. Since Immanuel Kant this motive has in general been designated as the theme of nature and freedom. Under the influence of the dogma of the autonomy of philosophical thought, its religious sense was camouflaged. Consequently, it was presented as a purely philosophical theme concerning the relation between theoretical and practical reason, a theme equally discussed in Greek and scholastic philosophy. In the same way, the Greek form-matter motive was presented in scholastic philosophy as a purely philosophical axiom concerning a primordial metaphysical distinction implied in the fundamental idea of being. A radical transcendental critique of philosophical thought should not be led astray by such axiomatic assertions. In fact, the Humanistic freedom-motive and its dialectical counterpart, the Humanist nature-motive, were of a central religious character.

The freedom-motive originated in a religion of humanity, into which the biblical basic-motive had been completely transformed. The renascimento device of the Italian Renaissance meant a real rebirth of man into a creative and entirely new personality. This personality was thought of as absolute in itself and was considered to be the only ruler of its own destiny and that of the world. This meant a Copernican revolution with respect to the biblical basic-motive of the Christian religion. The biblical revelation of the creation of [47] man in the image of God was implicitly subverted into the idea of a creation of God in the idealized image of man. The biblical conception of the rebirth of man and his radical freedom in Jesus Christ was replaced by the idea of a regeneration of man by his own autonomous will, his emancipation from the medieval kingdom of darkness, rooted in the belief of the supra-natural authority of the Church.

This new Humanistic freedom-motive, which was foreign to Greek thought since it presupposed the Christian motive of creation, fall into sin and redemption, called forth a new view of nature, which was con-

---

1   Summa Theologiae, Ia.1.8; In. Boeth., 2.3.
2   John Duns Scotus and William of Ockham.

ceived of as the macro-cosmic counterpart of the new, religious personality-ideal. This so-called discovery of nature, in the Renaissance, had an indubitable religious background. After having emancipated himself from all belief in a supra-natural sphere in its scholastic-ecclesiastical sense, and having made himself into the only master of his destiny, modern man seeks in nature infinite possibilities to satisfy his own creative impulse. He considers the macrocosm from the optimistic viewpoint of his own expectation of the future. This means that the scholastic conception of the divine creator as natura naturans is transferred to the new image of nature. The adage, Deus sive natura [God or nature], current in the Italian Renaissance, testifies to a deification of the new image of nature, which is radically different from the deification of the ever-flowing stream of life in the old Ionian philosophy of nature.

The revolution brought about later on by Copernicus [48] in the astronomic image of the universe, was considered by the rising Humanism to be a consequence of the religious revolution caused by the rebirth (renascimento) device of the Italian Renaissance. The modern autonomous man recreates both his divine Origin and his world in his own image.

But the new freedom-motive, just like its correlative, the new nature-motive, includes a diversity of possible tendencies. The reason is that it lacks the radical unity of sense proper to the biblical conception of Christian freedom, which concerns the true root and center of human existence. Much rather, it again diverts the concentric religious impulse of the human ego towards the temporal horizon of our experience with its diversity of modal aspects. This means that the Humanistic basic-motive does not imply a univocal answer to the question: Where is the central seat of man's autonomous liberty to be found? Neither does it furnish a univocal answer to the question: What is the relation between man's free and autonomous personality and the realm of nature, and, under which viewpoint can nature be conceived as a unity? From the Humanist starting-point, the center of man's autonomous and creative freedom might be sought in the moral, or in the aesthetic, in the theoretico-logical or in the sensitive aspect of our temporal experiential horizon. In the same way the unity of nature as the macrocosmic universe could be conceived under different absolutized modal viewpoints.

Nevertheless, there was from the very beginning a [49] strong tendency in the freedom-motive to strive after the rulership over nature, and this tendency, too, testifies to the influence of the secularized biblical creation-motive on the Humanist starting-point. For the biblical revelation concerning the creation of man in the image of God is immediately followed by the great cultural commandment that man should subject the earth and have the rule over it. As soon as the tendency to dominate the temporal world acquired the upperhand, in the Humanist freedom-motive, the central seat of man's autonomous freedom was sought in mathematical thought. In sharp contrast with the Greek and medieval conception of mathematics, a creative power was ascribed to mathematical analysis, viewed as the universal foundation of logic. The Humanist freedom-motive does not allow the acceptance of a given structural order of creation within the temporal horizon of experience. This would contradict the Humanist meaning of the autonomy of theoretical thought, which is fundamentally different both from the Greek and from the scholastic view of this autonomy. Therefore, the Cartesian renovation of the methodical fundamentals of philosophy implied a theoretical destruction of the entire given structural order of human experience, in order to reconstruct the material world more geometrico.[1]

The impulse to dominate nature by an autonomous scientific thought required a deterministic image of the world, construed as an uninterrupted chain of functional causal relations, to be formulated in [50] mathematical equations. Galileo and Newton laid the foundations of classical mathematical physics. To construct an image of the world corresponding with the domination-motive, the method of this special science was elevated to a universal pattern of scientific philosophic thought. Nature was conceived as a central unity under the absolutized mechanistic viewpoint. But now the inner religious dialectic of the Humanistic basic motive began to reveal itself in modern philosophy. The mechanistic world-image constructed under the primacy of the nature-motive, aiming at the sovereign domination of the world, left no room for the autonomous freedom of human personality in its practical activity. Nature and freedom appeared to be opposite motives in the Humanistic starting-point.

Henceforth, Humanistic philosophy was involved in a restless dialectical process. With Rousseau,[2] primacy is transferred to the freedom-motive and the central seat of human freedom is sought in the modal aspect of feeling. Kant's critical philosophy led to a sharp separation of the realms of nature and freedom.[3] The nature motives were depreciated. The mathematical and mechanistic science-ideal was restricted to an empirical world of sensory phenomena ordered by transcendental-logical categories of the human understanding. The autonomous freedom of man does not belong to the sensory realm of nature,

---

1   As Descartes explains in his *Synopsis* of the *Meditations*, "the only order which I could follow was that normally employed by geometers, namely to set out all the premises on which a desired proposition depends, before drawing any conclusions about it." Descartes, *Meditations on First Philosophy*, in *The Philosophical Writings of Descartes*, Volume II, eds. J. Cottingham, R. Stoothoff and D. Murdoch (Cambridge: Cambridge University Press, 1984), p. 9.

2   See, for example, Jean-Jacques Rousseau, *The Social Contract and Discourse on the Origin of Inequality*, ed. Lester G. Crocker (New York: Simon & Schuster, 1967).

3   While space is cleared for this distinction in the First Critique (*The Critique of Pure Reason*, A797-804/B825-832), it is most systematically considered in the Second Critique. See Kant, *Critique of Practical Reason*, Third Edition, trans. Lewis White Beck (New York: Prentice-Hall, 1993).

but to the supra-sensory realm of ethics, which is not ruled by natural laws, but by norms. As in Rousseau, the religious primacy was ascribed to the freedom-motive. [51] But the central seat of human freedom was now sought in the moral aspect of the human will. (Post-Kantian idealism[1] seeks to overcome Kant's critical dualism by a dialectical mode of thought which was supposed to bring about an ultimate synthesis of nature and freedom.)

The mathematical science-ideal, born from the impulse to dominate nature, is replaced by another philosophical pattern of thought, oriented to the historical aspect of experience. This gives rise to a historicist view of the temporal world, which reduces all the other aspects of our experience to the historical one. The new historical mode of thought is polarly opposed to the rationalistic and individualistic method of thinking, which originated from the mathematical and mechanistic science-idea. It is inspired by an irrationalistic and universalistic turn in the Humanist freedom-motive. But in the middle of the last century, the German freedom-idealism broke down and gave place to a naturalistic positivism. The nature-motive regained the upperhand and the historical mode of thought was transformed into a more complicated kind of natural scientific thinking. Meanwhile historicism, no longer checked by the belief in eternal ideas of the human reason, began to display its relativistic consequences, resulting in a process of spiritual uprooting of Western thought. The former Humanistic belief itself was viewed as a mere historical phenomenon, the perishable product of our Western cultural mind. The transitory influence of neo-Kantianism and neo-Hegelianism could not stop [52] this process. Both contemporary logical positivism and its polar opposite, Humanistic existentialism, testify to a fundamental crisis of Humanist philosophy.

§ 8.   The limits and possibility of philosophical dialogue

This brief survey of the central significance of the religious basic-motives of Western thought may suffice to show the necessity of a radical transcendental critique of philosophical thinking. The central influence of the religious motives upon philosophical thought is mediated by a threefold transcendental basic idea that, consciously or unconsciously, is laid to the foundation of any philosophical reflection and which alone makes such reflection possible. This threefold basic idea, which I have called the "cosmonomic idea" of philosophy,[2] is related to the three primordial transcendental basic problems concerning the theoretical attitude of thought as such, which we have formulated and considered in our first lecture [chapter one]. Consequently, it contains first a transcendental limiting idea of the whole of our temporal horizon of experience

---

1   Dooyeweerd is referring to Hegel.
2   See *NC* 1:93-113.

with its modal diversity of aspects, including a view of the mutual relation between these aspects; secondly, an idea of the central reference point of all synthetical acts of thought; and, in the third place, an idea of the Origin, whether or not it is called God, relating all that is relative to the absolute.

Though such a transcendental basic idea is a general and necessary condition of philosophical thought, [53] the positive content given to it is dependent upon the central basic motive which rules the thinking ego. This implies that even the transcendental critique of philosophy which I have briefly explained in these two lectures could not be independent of my own religious starting-point. This gives rise to two critical questions which you will doubtless ask me at the conclusion of my explanation. First: How can this criticism have any conclusive force for those who do not accept your religious starting-point? And, second: What may be the common basis for a philosophical discussion between those who lack a common starting-point?

a)   The transcendence of the world

As to the first question, I may reply that my analysis of theoretical thought had no other basic aim, than to lay bare the structural data of our temporal horizon of experience and of the theoretical attitude of thinking, both of which are of general validity. But I have also shown why these structural data were inevitably lost from sight as long as the dogma concerning the autonomy of theoretical reason impeded a radical transcendental critique of philosophical thought. Under the influence of unrecognized absolutizations of theoretical abstractions there arose a diversity of opposing philosophical views concerning human experience and empirical reality, lacking a truly critical verification. And the absolutizations, as it turned out, originated from dialectical basic-motives of a religious character. The radical biblical basic motive unmasks any absolutization of the relative, and may free philosophical thought from [54] dogmatic prejudices which impede an integral view of the real structures of human experience. This effect is verifiable since it manifests itself within the temporal experiential horizon, whose structural order has a general validity for every thinker.[1]

This certainly does not mean that our transcendental critique, since it starts from this radical basic motive, may lay claim to a philosophical

---

1   While theoretical thought is grounded in pretheoretical 'religious' commitments which determine interpretation, nevertheless the phenomena which theory seeks to explain are shared by all; that is, it is the same world which confronts these different 'schools.' Thus below Dooyeweerd emphasizes the "transcendental significance" of the world as given in experience which he describes as a "state of affairs," roughly equivalent to Husserl's *die Sache selbst* ['the things themselves']. Though the different philosophical 'schools' are grounded in different basic motives, because they 'share' this world, "verification" is possible because the structural order of the world

infallibility. This supposition would testify to a philosophical self-exaltation, which originates in the lack of true self-knowledge. Every philosophical reflection is a fallible human activity and a Christian philosophy has, in itself, no privileged position in this respect. It is only its biblical basic-motive that can give it a truly Christian character and free it from dogmatic prejudices which impede insight into the integral order of human experience founded in divine creation.

Structural data, founded in the temporal order of human experience, however, are facts of a transcendental significance, which should be acknowledged, irrespective of their philosophical interpretation. If these data seem not to agree with certain dogmatical presuppositions of a philosophical school, the adherents of the latter should not try to eliminate the data, but to find a satisfactory philosophical explanation upon the basis of their own starting-point. Every philosophical current may contribute to the testing of its own and other philosophical views with respect to data which, up to now, have been neglected. For the discovery of this neglected state of affairs in our experiential horizon is not the monopoly of a particular [55] philosophical school. Thanks to common grace,[1] relative truths are to be found in every philosophy, although the interpretation of such truths may appear to be unacceptable from the biblical standpoint insofar as the philosophical interpretation turns out to be ruled by a dialectical and apostate basic-motive. However, no philosophy can prosper in isolation.

b)   The basis for philosophical dialogue

Here I arrive at the second question: What may be the common basis for a philosophical discussion between those who do not share a common starting-point? I think the first condition for finding such a common basis should be the conviction that any serious philosophical current has to contribute in its own way to the fulfillment of the common philosophical task of mankind. This conviction should be at the foundation of every philosophical debate even if the views concerning the task of philosophy may diverge to a high degree, and, even though the philosophical basic ideas have been ruled by unbiblical motives and hence, have been fundamentally erroneous. Therefore, the barren exclusivistic atti-

---

is binding on every interpretation (cp. Heidegger, *Being and Time*, § 44). For a fuller discussion, see *NC* 2:542-582.

1   This notion of 'common grace' is central to the Christian appropriation of and dialogue with non-Christian thought. In De Doctrina Christiana (II.xlv.60-xlvii.63), Augustine speaks of the recovery of philosophical truth from pagans as the 'spoils of Egypt' which "we should claim back for our own use...as from its unjust oppressors" who have themselves mined this gold of Truth from "the ore of divine providence." Thus, whatever is found to be true in non-Christian philosophy must be attributed to the "common grace" of the one Teacher of all. See also Calvin, Institutes, II.ii.13-17.

tude of the schools, in which each of them was supposed to have the monopoly of philosophical truth, should be broken down.

The chief cause of this exclusivism was the dogmatic absolutization of specific patterns of thought and the lack of insight into the central influence of the supratheoretical basic motives on the inner philosophical attitude of thought. Therefore the radical transcendental critique of theoretical thought, which [56] I have developed in these two lectures, is, in my opinion, of a universal value for all students of philosophy. For the three transcendental basic problems of philosophical thought which it has formulated cannot be evaded by any philosopher who wishes, indeed, to think critically. The reason is that they originate in the inner nature of the theoretical attitude of thought itself, which is one and the same for every thinker. Every philosophical current should try to solve them from its own starting-point, but this starting-point should no longer be camouflaged by the multivocal dogma concerning the autonomy of theoretical thought.

The first result of a participation of all philosophical trends in the radical transcendental critique of theoretical thought will be that it paves the way for a real discussion between philosophers who have different starting-points, or who have arrived at polarly opposed positions while rooted in the same dialectical basic motive. Those who participate in such a discussion should penetrate to each other's supratheoretical presuppositions in order to be able to exercise a truly immanent criticism of each other's philosophical views. Then they will also be prepared to learn from one another by testing their divergent philosophical conceptions of the empirical world by the real states of affairs within the structural order of human experience, which order is a common condition of every philosophy.

The continual confrontation of the different philosophical [57] views of experience with these structural data on the one hand, and with the supratheoretical starting-points on the other, will introduce a new critical mind of mutual understanding into the philosophical debate.

One of the first structural data of human experience within the order of time which our new critique of theoretical thought has brought to light is the fundamental modal diversity of this experience and the inter-relation of the different experiential modes. It is true that my explanation of this structural state of affairs was from the very beginning ruled by my transcendental basic Idea which implied the mutual irreducibility of the experiential modes, in their very interrelation. And it is also true that this transcendental Idea is in turn ruled by the biblical basic motive, which unmasks, in principle, every absolutization of a relative mode of the temporal order. But this does not detract from the fact that my transcendental view of the mutual relation between the fundamental modes of experience is capable of verification by those who do not share my starting-point. This verification may occur by confronting this view with states of affairs relating to the general basic concepts of the different special sciences, which imply a theoretical synthesis of the logical and the different non-logical experiential modes. These basic concepts contain, undoubtedly, analogical moments in which the inner coherence of the different modes of experience finds expression. From a logical positivistic [58] standpoint, this state of affairs has even led to the suggestion of a unification of the basic concepts of the different special sciences. However, as soon as we try to reduce a fundamental experiential mode to another, our theoretical thought is entangled in unsolvable antinomies.[1]

Some of these antinomies were already known in ancient Greek thought. I refer, for instance, to the antinomies which arise from the attempt to reduce the experiential mode of extensive movement to the spatial mode of experience. Extensive movement implies a spatial analogy, namely, that of extension. But this extensive movement is qualified by the nuclear moment of the aspect of movement, namely that of continuous flowing, while spatial extension is of a static character.

The antinomies which result in theoretical thought from disregarding the irreducible nature of the fundamental experiential modes show that there are structural states of affairs in our experience which cannot be neglected with impunity. These states of affairs can, indeed, furnish a common basis for every philosophical discussion since they are transcendental data and as such have a general validity for every philosophy.

In the new critique of philosophical thought, whose principal traits I explained in these two lectures, the tracing of theoretical antinomies has been elaborated into a systematical method of immanent criticism of the philosophical systems. This method may be used to test every philosophical total view of [59] our experiential horizon by the structural data of the latter within the temporal order.

Naturally this immanent criticism is not able to put an end to the contest between the different philosophical views of human experience and empirical reality. The reason is that the structural data referred to above can be of a nature that lead to different philosophical interpretations in accordance with the different transcendental basic ideas which lie at the foundation of the latter. As a result, even the antinomies may be philosophically interpreted in a different sense. Those who ignore the fundamental modal diversity of the temporal order of experience and hold to the autonomy of theoretical human reason in its Humanistic sense may

---

1 On these 'antinomies, see *NC* 2:570ff.

try to reduce them to merely logical contradictions. In his Critique of Pure Reason Kant, too, did so.[1]

The central influence of the different religious basic motives upon philosophical thought is here clearly revealed. It was the very aim of our transcendental critique to show why this ultimate difference cannot be eliminated from the philosophical discussion. And I think the factual state of affairs, as it presents itself in the average debate between different philosophical trends, corroborates the results of this critique. Does this mean that we should abandon the belief in a transcendental standard of truth which has general validity with respect to the philosophical total views of our experiential horizon and of the empirical world? Does, in other words, our transcendental critique of philosophical thought result in a [60] general theoretical relativism by making the philosophical standard of truth dependent upon the different transcendental basic Ideas? No, this would be a fundamental misunderstanding of the real intention of this criticism.

The structural temporal order of our experience, to which our critique has continually appealed, cannot be dependent upon the subjective transcendental basic Ideas, since it is a transcendental condition of philosophical thought itself. We have emphatically established that every state of affairs which is founded in this structural temporal order is a transcendental datum for every philosophical theory, and that each philosophical total view of experience is to be tested by these data. It is true that the latter may be interpreted in different philosophical ways; but this does not mean that the philosophical interpretations are withdrawn from a general standard of truth.[2]

These philosophical interpretations turn out to be misinterpretations insofar as they amount to a reasoning away of structural data of our experience. Such a reasoning away may result from devotion to a closed and consistently carried through philosophical system. This is a danger to which every philosopher is subjected, irrespective of his religious starting-point. It shows the necessity of a really critical discussion between the different philosophical trends. But it may also be that the disregarding of essential transcendental data of our experience is caused by the religious basic motive of a philosophical school which prompts philosophical thought to absolutizations as long as it is in that basic motive's central grip. [61] This is why the transcendental standard of truth,

---

1 Kant, *Critique of Pure Reason*, Transcendental Dialectic, esp. A405-461/B432-489.

2 For Dooyeweerd, Truth is not an objective 'thing' but rather a *process* by which the structural states of affairs are 'uncovered' or 'disclosed.' For his development of this "perspective structure of truth," see *NC* 2:571-582. For an analogous treatment (which likely even functions as a source for Dooyeweerd), see Heidegger, *Being and Time*, § 44.

which is bound to the temporal structural order of our experience, is dependent on the transcendent, religious standard by which alone the central starting points of philosophy can be tested. This truly absolute standard of truth is not to be found in man, but only in the Word of God, in its central sense, which uncovers the source of all absolutizations and which alone can lead man to true knowledge of himself and of his absolute Origin.

PART TWO

Historicism and the Sense of History

Chapter Three

The Evolution of Historicism

§ 9. Historicism as an absolutization of the historical aspect

At great turning-points of world-history, man's historical consciousness is strongly aroused. The relativity of our traditional measures and opinions manifests itself in a clear way. At these historical turning points those who do not live by the Word of God and who had considered these traditional measures and opinions to be the firm ground of their personal and societal life, easily fall prey to a state of spiritual uprooting, in which they surrender themselves to a radical relativism, which has lost all faith in an absolute truth.

If this state of uprooting remains restricted to a transitional phase and does not consolidate into a mass-phenomenon which finds expression in a consistently carried through life and world view, it may be soon overcome. But when it turns out to have a deeper cause than the breakdown of the belief in tradition and to be the result of a process of increasing undermining of the ultimate spiritual fundamentals of a whole civilization, we may rightly speak of a fundamental crisis of the latter.

One of the most alarming symptoms of the beginning of a fundamental crisis of Western culture since the last decades of the 19th century was the rise of a radically historicist world- and life-view. This view leaves no other perspective than a spiritual nihilism, whose motto is: "Let us eat and drink, for tomorrow we die."

Radical historicism makes the historical viewpoint the all-encompassing one, absorbing all the other aspects of the human experiential horizon.[1] Even the religious center of human experience, the human ego or selfhood, [63] is reduced to a flowing stream of historical moments of consciousness. All our scientific, philosophical, ethical, aesthetic, political and religious standards and conceptions are viewed as the expression of the mind of a particular culture or civilization. Each civilization has arisen and ripened in the all-embracing stream of historical development. Once its florescence has ended, it is destined to decline. And it is merely dogmatical illusion to think that man would be able to view his world and life from another standpoint than the historical. History has no windows looking out into eternity. Man is completely enclosed in it and cannot elevate himself to a supra-historical level of contemplation.

---

1   In this way historicism is a form of 'absolutization' of a single aspect of temporal experience. Dooyeweerd engages historicism as one contemporary form of 'idolatry' (as that word is used in its technical sense discussed earlier).

45

History is the be-all and end-all of man's existence and of his faculty of experience. And it is ruled by destiny, the inescapable fate.

This was the radical historicism developed in Oswald Spengler's famous work, The Decline of the West.[1] According to him, our Western culture is doomed to decline, and nothing can save it, since it has finished its fatal course in history. This work, published soon after the end of the first world-war and written in a brilliant style, made a deep impression. In many respects it prepared the way for the flood-tide of the so-called existentialist philosophical movement, which acquired a dominant position in European thought, especially since the second World War. In existentialism, the historicist view is exclusively concentrated upon the human selfhood and its place in the world. But the underlying pessimistic [64] tone of Spengler's view of human historical existence is clearly maintained. Destiny, concern and anxiety, death and human failure, night without dawn, – these are the ruling themes of this philosophy in so far as it holds to a purely historicist viewpoint. Toynbee's voluminous work on world-history also clearly reveals the influence of Spengler's ideas.[2] However, it may be observed that this English writer tries to break through Spengler's fatalism by positing his expectation of an ultimate revival of true Christendom. Only such a revival, according to Toynbee, will be able to save Western culture from its destiny of decline.

§ 10   The origins of historicism in modern philosophy

It should be noted that from the outset historicism did not display the radical character that we observe in Spengler. It originated in the first half of the last century, in the period of the so-called Restoration. With an idealistic philosophy, it placed the historical mode of thought in opposition to the mathematical and natural science pattern of thinking which had ruled the philosophical picture of world and life in the preceding period since Descartes. To be more precise we should mention that the rise of a moderate historicism dates from the 18th century. In fact, it was the Italian philosopher, Vico, who was the first to set the historical model of science in opposition to the mathematical Cartesian science ideal.[3] However, the historicist world-view in general did not gain ground over against the anti-historical world-picture of the preceding period until the time of the Restoration.

---

1   Oswald Spengler, The Decline of the West, 2 Vols., trans. Charles Francis Atkinson (New York: Knopf, 1928). With regard to the question of historicism, it is important to note that Spengler's thought represents a certain Nietzschean heritage.

2   Arnold Toynbee, A Study of History, 10 Vols. (Oxford: Oxford University Press, 1934).

3   Giambattista Vico, The New Science in Vico: Selected Writings, ed. and trans. Leon Pompa (Cambridge: Cambridge University Press, 1982).

What was the background of this opposition? Modern philosophy, [65] founded by the French thinker Descartes, had a hidden starting-point which was radically different from that of the medieval scholastic philosophy of Thomas Aquinas. The latter had been accepted as the rational foundation of the Roman Catholic doctrine. But the Cartesian philosophy, though its founder sought to avoid every direct conflict with the church, was in fact ruled by the religious basic motive of the Humanistic movement which had originated from the time of the Italian Renaissance. This Renaissance was, in the first place, a religious movement, aiming at a transformation of the Christian religion into a religion of the human personality and of humanity. It required a real rebirth of the human being not in its biblical sense, but in the sense of its regeneration into a completely free and autonomous personality, the sole ruler of its own destiny and that of the world. The central biblical theme of creation, fall into sin, and redemption by Jesus Christ in the communion of the Holy Spirit, was indeed reinterpreted in the sense of this Humanistic freedom-motive. Relying on his natural reason alone, man supposedly could recreate his world and his god in his own image. This Copernican revolution, which the Humanistic freedom-motive had brought about in the biblical view of man's creation in the image of God, called up a new religious view of nature as the macrocosmically reflected image of the free and emancipated human personality. The "discovery of nature" by the Renaissance man brought about a new religious attitude towards the world which also needed liberation [66] from the ecclesiastical view of creation, sin and miracles.

This central religious basic motive of modern Humanism may be correctly designated as that of nature and freedom. Since the famous German philosopher Immanuel Kant, this denomination has generally been accepted to indicate the central theme which ruled the Humanist world- and life-view, but which in fact was its religious starting point. This motive was radically different from that of medieval scholastic philosophy since Thomas Aquinas, namely, that of nature and supra-natural grace. This latter motive invovled that there is a natural sphere in creation which can be known by the natural light of human reason alone, but that this sphere is subordinated to a supernatural sphere of grace which is only known by divine revelation, entrusted to the Church. Therefore, natural reason should not contradict the supernatural truths of the doctrine of the Church. In this way medieval philosophy was subjected to ecclesiastical control. This scholastic motive of nature and grace, which entered Roman Catholic doctrine, deprived the central theme of the Word-revelation – namely, that of creation, fall into sin and redemption by Jesus Christ in the communion of the Holy Spirit – of its radical and integral character. By accepting a natural sphere of life, which was supposed to be related to the human intellect alone and apart from any religious presupposition, it paved the way for a philosophy which did not acknowledge any other authority than human reason. [67]

Humanist philosophy eliminated the so-called supra-natural sphere. Nor would it accept a given world-order founded in divine creation. This was incompatible with its religious basic-motive which implied the absolute autonomy of human reason. It could not accept any order of the world that does not originate from the autonomous and free human reason itself. Therefore, the Cartesian philosophy started with a methodical, theoretical destruction of the world as it presents itself in the given order of human experience. After this methodical destruction of the given world, only the thinking human ego with its innate mathematical ideas is left. And this thinking ego, which seeks the criterion of truth only in itself, sets itself the task of recreating the world in the image of its mathematical pattern of thought.

We encounter the same Humanist transformation of the biblical idea of creation in the philosophy of Descartes' younger British contemporary, Thomas Hobbes. In the foreword of his work, De Corpore[1] (on the corporeal world), in which he explains his philosophy of nature, Hobbes says that philosophy should begin with a methodical destruction of the given world. With a clear allusion to the first chapter of the book of Genesis, he suggests that after this methodical experiment logical thought should command: "Let there be light!" And this allusion is corroborated by the following explanation: "For logical thought should create, like God or like the artist." To achieve this rule of the world of nature by creative, autonomous thought alone, both Descartes [68] and Hobbes projected a picture of the world in accordance with a strictly mathematical and mechanical pattern. This picture of nature did not leave any room for the autonomous freedom of man in his practical activity within the world. For as a corporeal, natural being, man was supposed to be subjected to the same mechanical causality which ruled this image of nature as a whole. To save human freedom, which was supposed to have its center in mathematical thought, Descartes suggested that the human soul, conceived of as a thinking substance, should be considered philosophically as if no body existed, and vice versa. But Hobbes did not acknowledge this limitation of the mechanical world-image. The rational soul, too, should be considered as a mechanism.

So the Humanist basic motive of nature and freedom began to display its inner conflict and dialectical tension. The mechanistic idol of nature, evoked by the Humanist freedom-motive itself, turned out to be a true

---

1   In The English Works of Thomas Hobbes, ed. Sir William Moleworth (Oxford: Oxford University Press, 1962).

Leviathan (the legendary monster mentioned in the book of Job), which threatened to devour the idol of the free and autonomous humanity. This conflict was, consequently, not of a merely theoretical, philosophical character. Rather, it originated in the central religious starting-point of Humanist thought. Hence it did not allow a real solution to be found from within the Humanist standpoint itself. The only way out was the ascription of the primacy, or the religious precedence, to one of the two opposing motives, either to that of the rule over nature, or to that of practical human freedom; with the result, naturally, that the other itself was depreciated. [69]

§ 11. The dialectical tension in modern humanism

a) The primacy of nature: Descartes, Hobbes and Leibniz

The continual shifting of the primacy from the one motive to the other caused a dialectical process in modern Humanistic thought, which drove it in polarly opposite directions, from the naturalistic pole to that of freedom-idealism, and vice versa. The ascription of the primacy to the nature-motive meant, indeed, a cult of mathematical and natural scientific thought, which was supposed to be capable of creating an image of nature as it really is, in contradistinction to that which presents itself in the given order of human experience. The cult of this science-ideal implied also an idea of the divine creator constructed in the image of this pattern of thought. For this reason the great German philosopher Leibniz, called God the great Geometer. His discovery of differential and integral calculus called up in his religious consciousness the idol of a divine mathematician able to carry through this admirable method of mathematical analysis to such an extent that it would even make calculable the chance occurrences.

So long as this mathematical science-ideal had the primacy in modern philosophy, even human society was constructed after its pattern. The given societal order, which still showed many remnants of the medieval feudal regime, did not satisfy the Humanist view of human autonomy. Thus, this societal order, too, was subjected to a methodical destruction by theoretical thought. It was dissolved into its supposed elemental components, i.e. the free and equal individuals who were assumed to have existed in a pre-societal state of nature. Using these elements, philosophical [70] thought could freely create a theoretical image of human society corresponding to the Humanist mathematical science-ideal, which aims at complete control over the temporal world. The first concern was to construct a body politic, provided with absolute power over all other societal relationships, in order to dissolve all connection with medieval society. To this end, the state was defined as an artificial body characterized by its absolute sovereignty but exclusive of any internal sphere sovereignty[1] of non-political institutions such as the family and the church. To make this absolute sovereignty acceptable, it was adapted to the Humanist idea of the autonomous freedom of man, by the construction of a general and reciprocal social contract between individuals, whether or not this was accompanied by a second contract with the instituted sovereign government. By this compact, the individuals were supposed to have abandoned their natural freedom by their own autonomous will and to have transferred all power to the instituted sovereign government. The validity of this compact was derived from a natural law principle: namely, that agreements are to be kept; a principle which was assumed to be founded in autonomous human reason. Notwithstanding this formal concession to the Humanist freedom-ideal, however, it was clear that the State Leviathan, construed after the mathematical pattern of thought, absorbed all human freedom. Here, too, the inner conflict in the Humanist basic motive of nature and freedom was clearly revealed. [71] Political theory, the theory of law, and the entire view of human society was, in this period, quite anti-historical.

b) *The primacy of freedom: Locke, Rousseau and Kant*

The supremacy of the mathematical science-ideal could not fail to evoke a strong reaction on the part of the threatened freedom-motive. The shifting of the religious primacy to the latter motive had already made itself known in the 18th century, in a fundamental criticism of Cartesian philosophy, and in the rise of the doctrine of innate and inalienable human rights and of the liberal state-idea, which were both developed by John Locke. Rousseau openly discounted the mathematical science-ideal and proclaimed the absolute precedence of the ideal of practical human freedom. Kant, who was strongly influenced by him, depreciated the scientific image of nature by restricting it to the world of sense phenomena. According to him, freedom and volitional autonomy of the human personality do not belong to the world of nature but to the supra-sensory kingdom of ethics, which does not relate to what is but what ought to be. Human freedom is an idea of practical reason, which can neither be proved nor refuted by scientific thought since the latter is restricted to the sensory world of nature. One should believe in the freedom of human personality since our practical reason commands us to do so, and since practical reason has the absolute primacy.[2]

---

1 Dooyeweerd inherits the notion of "sphere sovereignty" from Abraham Kuyper, who emphasized that social institutions such as the state, family, and church, all have distinct 'spheres' of authority which are grounded in creational diversity and must remain distinct in order to allow proper development or "differentiation." For further explanation, see Glossary (p.139) and Wolters, "The Intellectual Milieu of Herman Dooyeweerd," pp. 5-6.

2 Thus Kant's famous dictum: "I have therefore found it necessary to deny knowledge, in order to make room for faith" (Critique of Pure Reason, p. xxx).

This shifting of the primacy to the freedom-motive requires, as its correlate, also a Humanist idea of God. The Kantian god is no longer the divine Geometer; [72] rather he has become the deified image of the autonomous and free human personality in its ethical aspect. The idea of God is, according to Kant, a requirement of practical human reason – that is to say, of an autonomous ethics. There ought to be a God, able to recompense human virtue with eternal beatitude, since in the present life moral human freedom and autonomy can only be realized at the cost of man's natural happiness.[1]

Thus the inner conflict between the nature-motive and the freedom-motive in the religious starting-point of Humanism led Kant to a strongly dualistic world- and life-view. Nature and freedom were sharply separated from one another, which corresponded to Kant's separation between science and faith, which consequently had a religious background. But the ascription of the religious primacy to the freedom-motive did not immediately give rise to another pattern of scientific thought to replace the mathematical and natural scientific view of Descartes and Hobbes. So long as the individualistic and rationalistic view of human personality in its social relationships was not abandoned, the influence of the mathematical science-ideal was not completely overcome. Both Rousseau and Kant continued to construct human society in a mathematical way, from its supposed elements (namely, the abstract human individuals, in their presumed natural freedom and equality).

The rationalistic trait in Kantian ethics, testifying to the continued influence of the mathematical [73] science-ideal upon him, comes to the fore in his conception of the autonomy of man's ethical will. The true autos (i.e., selfhood of man) is, according to him, identical with the general formula of the nomos (i.e., the ethical Law or categorical imperative), which his practical reason prescribes to him. The pure ethical will was supposed to have no other motivation than respect for this general law. There was no room left for the individuality of the human person in this legalistic ethics. As an abstract individual, every person was considered to be nothing but a specimen of this general normative idea of human personality. Therefore Kant lacked the insight into a real community as a social whole, which is not identical with the sum of the individuals, but brings about an inner inter-relation between its members.

c) *A dialectical synthesis: post-Kantian idealism*

However, in the period of the Restoration, after the liquidation of the French Revolution, the Humanistic freedom-motive began to reveal itself in a new version of the development of post-Kantian idealist phi-

---

1   See Kant, Critique of Practical Reason, pp. 130-138 ("The Existence of God as a Postulate of Pure Practical Reason").

losophy.[1] The Kantian belief in the eternal normative idea of a free and autonomous mankind was maintained; but the legalistic view of the ideal human personality, willing to conform himself to the general rule of the ethical law, was rejected. It was no longer the general law which determined the true selfhood of man, but the reverse was said to be true. The ethical rule of behavior could only be derived from the concrete individuality of the human personality, from its individual disposition and task in the world. This was the irrationalistic counter-part of Kant's [74] rationalistic view of human autonomy. Rationalism seeks to eliminate the irreducible individuality of the human subject by reducing its true selfhood to a general law of man's practical reason. The irrationalistic view, on the contrary, rejects every general law as a falsification of true reality, and it absolutizes the incomparable subjective individuality of human personality.

To evade the anarchical consequences of this ethical irrationalism, Romanticism and post-Kantian idealism bound it to the idea of human community,[2] especially to the idea of the national community, which had strongly come to the fore in the Napoleontic wars. This meant that the Humanist freedom idea was now applied to man in the context of national community. Abstract individuals, so it was argued, do not exist. Every man is born into the community of a nation, which determines his individual character, while the communal will at the same time determines his own autonomous will. The nation is a temporal revelation of the eternal idea of humanity, of a spiritual community. Every nation has its own individual mind, its Volksgeist. It brings forth its own culture in autonomous, creative freedom, including its own political organization, its own language, its own customs, its own legal order, its own fine arts, and so forth. General patterns of political constitutions and law, of moral and aesthetic standards, etc., which are appropriate for all peoples and for every era, as the rationalistic philosophy of the French Revolution imagined, do not exist. The individual national [75] mind creates its culture, including all its social institutions and rules, in a long process of historical development. This development is one of autonomous freedom without being arbitrary. On the contrary, it has creative power, which operates in conformity to a hidden natural necessity, so that the historical development of a national culture is an organic process, which

---

1 Hegel and Schelling would be primary representatives of post-Kantian German idealism. Schelling is discussed specifically below, but Hegel stands behind much of what Dooyeweerd describes here.

2 This is what Hegel describes as Sittlichkeit (in contrast to Kant's Moralität): the production of ethics from the community and the embodiment of ethics in the community. See Hegel, Phenomenology of the Spirit, trans. A.V. Miller (Oxford: Oxford University Press, 1977), pp. 266-409.

is sharply distinguished from all revolutionary mechanical and artificial modes of cultural fabrication.

What is the meaning of the process of historical development having been conceived here as a combination of autonomous freedom and natural necessity? Post-Kantian idealism was not satisfied with Kant's critical separation between nature and freedom. It sought to overcome the inner conflict in the religious starting-point of Humanism by a so-called dialectical mode of thought, which was supposed to bring about a synthesis between the opposite motives of nature and freedom. To do this, the mathematical and mechanical image of nature, constructed by the Cartesian philosophy, had to be abandoned. The famous German philosopher, Schelling, proclaimed the identity of nature and the free spirit as two forms of appearance of the absolute.[1] Nature, he held, should be viewed after the pattern of a living organism, developing itself into many forms from different potencies. He conceived of the organic process of nature as developing into ever higher forms as the unconscious operation of the world-spirit, whose free creative power works at the same time as a natural necessity. This organic development of nature is continued on a higher level [76] in the historical development of the national minds, which he conceived of as the spiritual potencies of human culture. In this historical process the creative freedom of the nations manifests itself also in conformity to a natural necessity which gives to this process an organic character. It is the individual nature of a nation which unfolds itself with this inner necessity. History does not know general laws. Nevertheless, according to Schelling, there lies a hidden law at the foundation of the organic development of a culture. As a gift of Providence, every national mind contains the Schicksal, or destiny of the national culture which originates from it.

The founders of the historical school,[2] having been thoroughly influenced by this romanticist world-view, began to develop a new historical pattern of scientific thought, which was sharply opposed to the mathematical and mechanistic mode of natural science. This new model of thought was applied in jurisprudence, political theory, economics, aesthetics and linguistics. After this pattern they designed a historicist image of reality, which soon was generally accepted as an axiom. Even many leading Christian thinkers and politicians welcomed this historicist view, especially in its application to human society, as a powerful ally in their contest against the principles of the French Revolution.

1 F.W.J. Schelling, Of Human Freedom, trans. James Gutmann (Chicago: Open Court, 1936), pp. 91-93.
2 A generally German intellectual movement in the late 18th and early 19th centuries (alongside romanticism and post-Kantian idealism) through which emerged "historical consciousness" and the development of historiography as a science.

They did not realize that this historicism was rooted in the same human-istic religious basic motive which had also ruled the philosophic ideas of Rousseau and his revolutionary disciples.

But we should not lose sight of the fact that the [77] radical conse-quences of this new view of reality could not yet become apparent so long as they were held in check by the firm belief in eternal values or ideas, which realize themselves in the temporal order of the historical process in a wealth of individual national forms. Thus it is understand-able that the Christian thinkers who joined the Historical School were of the opinion that this view was more biblical than the rationalistic phi-losophy of the fathers of the French Revolution. What else, so they ar-gued, is the Bible, other than the revelation of God's eternal plan in his-tory? Especially the irrationalistic view that the organic development of history occurs in accordance with a hidden Providence seemed to be quite congenial to the Christian belief in God's guidance in history. This hidden law of history could not fail to be interpreted in an irrationalistic normative sense as a rule for human behavior. And it was the Lutheran legal philosopher, Fr. Julius Stahl,[1] who openly accepted this conclu-sion. In his opinion, all that has come to pass in the long process of his-torical development, under the influence of incalculable and inscrutable forces without the interference of rational human planning, ought to be respected as a manifestation of God's guidance in history, insofar as it does not contradict God's revealed law. This view of God's providence in history was quite in accordance with the conservative mind of the Restoration, and it had a great influence upon the entire so-called Christian-historical, or anti-revolutionary movement in Germany, the Netherlands and [78] France. Stahl, too, had a strong belief in eternal ideas, which he conceived in a christianized sense as ideas of the divine world-order realizing themselves in history.

But the historicist world-picture had the inner tendency to undermine this belief. As soon as the idealist philosophy which had created it broke down, the historicist mode of thought began in an increasing degree to reveal its radical consequences. What else, so it was argued, is human belief itself other than the historical product of a particular cultural mind? What else are the so-called eternal ideas but ideas derived from our Western civilization, reflecting the particular course of its historical development?

Nevertheless, as long as the development of Western civilization con-tinued to be considered the center and standard of world-history, the radical form of historicism, which we encounter in Oswald Spengler, was out of the question. For this view, which was common both to the

---

1   Fr. Julius Stahl, Philosophie des Rechts nach geschichtlicher Ansicht [Philosophy of Law in Historical Perspective].

historical philosophy of the period of Enlightenment and to that of the post-Kantian freedom-idealism, incorporated the firm belief in a particular historical vocation of Western culture. This vocation implied that in the process of its development, Western civilization would reach an ultimate stage, in which the final aim of the entire world-history would be realized. And this final aim itself was withdrawn from the historicist relativization of all measures and values. The belief in either a steady, straight-lined, or in a dialectically conceived progress of mankind in its historical development was inherent in this view. [79] And even after its emancipation from idealist philosophy, the historicist view of the world and of life generally continued to be held in check by this belief until the breakdown of that belief brought into the open the fundamental crisis of Western civilization. Henceforth, Western culture was no longer viewed as the center of world-history, but as a particular civilization on the same footing as the Arabian, Indian, Chinese and other cultures.

§ 12. Radical historicism: from Comte to Dilthey to Spengler

Meanwhile, the transition from the inconsistent to the consistent, or radical, historicism was only a question of time. This transition started as soon as the idealistic foundation of the historical mode of thought was itself submitted to an historical explanation. The French thinker, August Comte, the founder of modern sociology, was the first to subject both the Christian belief and the Humanistic belief in the so-called eternal ideas of human reason to the historicist view.[1] With him the idealistic philosophical position was replaced by a positivistic one. This meant, in fact, the restoration of the supremacy of the natural scientific mode of thought, but in such a way that the new historicist view of human society was retained. The latter should only be adapted to the general pattern of natural scientific research which seeks to explain empirical facts by tracing the general laws of their causal inter-relations. Thus Comte attempted to trace the general law of the social history of mankind. And he clearly realized that this attempt was ruled by the old Humanistic motive to dominate both nature and the social world [80] by autonomous scientific thought; thus, he formulated his famous law of the three stages. According to it, human history proceeds from a theological to a metaphysical stage, and from the latter to a positivistic one. Each of them is ruled by particular ideas, corresponding to a particular type of society. The theological ideas, inclusive of Christian doctrine, must necessarily make room for the metaphysical ideas. The latter in-

---

1 August Comte's major work which unveiled this thesis was his Cours de philosophie positive, 6 Vols. (Paris: Bachelier, 1830-42), translated as The Positive Philosophy of Auguste Comte, Freely translated and condensed, by Harriet Martineau, 2 Vols. (1853).

cludes both the supposed eternal ideas of the rationalistic Humanist doctrine of natural law and those of its antipode, the idealistic metaphysics of history. These, in turn, must necessarily to be overcome by positivistic, or scientific man.[1]

But this historicist relativizing of the belief in eternal ideas was not yet carried through in a radical sense. For the last stage of human history is, according to Comte, the very aim of the entire historical process. It is the stage of a new humanity, which in complete freedom and autonomy rules the world, having developed to the highest level of social solidarity, welfare and morality, supplemented with a new Humanistic religion. In other words, Comte held to a strong belief in the future of mankind. The ideas of his positivist philosophy, evolved in the development of Western civilization, are to his mind, of a truly eternal value. And the idea of the steady and straight-lined progress of mankind by the autonomous power of science, which was characteristic of the period of the Enlightenment, lay at the foundation of his entire view of history.

Marxism, the source of contemporary Communism, gave to the idealist and dialectical historicist [81] world-view of Hegel a materialistic turn. According to Marx, all human ideas, inclusive of religious doctrines, are nothing but the ideological reflection of a particular technical system of economic production which arises, ripens and breaks down in the course of history with an inner dialectical necessity. Nevertheless, Marx was no more radical a historicist than was Comte – for he too was strongly committed to the belief in an eschatological consummation of history: the final redemption and liberation of mankind by the suffering proletariat, which will set in motion an earthly paradise of a classless communistic society after the destruction of capitalism. This Humanistic transformation of the Messianic[2] faith became the gospel of international communism, which founded its Jerusalem in Moscow, after the Russian revolution.

However, the radical Historicism, which began to undermine the spiritual fundamentals of our Western civilization since the last decades of the 19th century, has not retained any positive belief. The famous German philosopher and historian, Wilhelm Dilthey, who in many respects was one of its most brilliant apostles, said that it would lead hu-

---

1 And precisely as Dooyeweerd's theory would suggest, this commitment to positivism is in fact religious in nature. See Comte, The Catechism of Positive Religion, trans. R. Congreve (1858).

2 It is interesting to note that Dooyeweerd perceived the 'messianic' dimensions of Marxism at this time. The same has been suggested more recently by Jacques Derrida in Specters of Marx, trans. Peggy Kamuf (New York: Routledge, 1993). Derrida is following the work of critical theorist Walter Benjamin, "Theses on the Philosophy of History," in Illuminations, trans. Harry Zohn (New York: Harcourt, Brace & World, 1968).

manity to the highest level of freedom, since it liberates our mind from the last remnants of dogmatical prejudices.[1] But at his seventieth birthday he added something to this eulogy which clearly testified to his fear of the nihilistic apparition he had evoked. "Yes," said he, "historicism has freed the mind from the last remnants of dogmatism. But who will check the radical relativism which it has brought forth?"[2]

Historicism, whose rise and evolution we have [82] briefly sketched, appears to exercise a magical influence upon those who have come under its spell. From the very beginning it displayed a strongly aesthetical trait. Schelling ascribed to the entire process of history an aesthetical aim, namely, the production of the perfect work of fine art, in which nature and creative freedom were supposed to find their ultimate synthesis. We have also seen that in its initial irrationalistic form the historicist view captivated many Christian thinkers. But it should be noted that it is exactly the irrationalistic current in Historicism which, since the breakdown of the Humanist freedom-idealism, has resulted in the radical relativism of Spengler and his followers. The rationalistic trend, in the footsteps of August Comte, sought to trace general laws of history. This view, which found many adherents in Anglo-Saxon countries, never carried the historicist view through to its ultimate conclusions. However, the rationalistic form of historicism in general did not attract Christian thinkers, but it rather repelled them, especially after it joined up with Darwinian evolutionism.

This should prompt us to ask the question: "What is the snare in the historicist view of our temporal world in both of its forms?" And, "what is the real place and meaning of the historical aspect in the temporal order of our experience?" We shall try to answer these questions in our second lecture on this subject [chapter four].

---

1 For a representative work, see Wilhelm Dilthey, Introduction to the Human Sciences, Selected Works, Volume 1, eds. Rudolf Makkreel and Frithjof Rodi (Princeton: Princeton University Press, 1989).

2 Dooyeweerd is here paraphrasing the speech Dilthey delivered on his seventieth birthday, entitled "Der Traum [The Dream]," published in English in The Philosophy of History in Our Time, ed. Hans Meyerhoff (Garden City, NY: Doubleday, 1949, pp. 37-43. Dooyeweerd refers to the same, or at least similar remark in the NC: "The historical world-view has broken the last chain not yet broken by philosophy and natural science. Everything is flowing, nothing remains. But what are the means to conquer the anarchy of opinions which threatens us?" (2:207).

Chapter Four

Historicism, History, and the Historical Aspect

§ 13. The relation of the historical aspect and other modes of experience

a)   Historicism's absolutization of the historical aspect

In the previous lecture [chapter three] I tried to give a brief outline of the development of modern Historicism and its spiritual background. If the historicist view is restricted to our temporal world and is not turned against the supra-temporal religious sphere of truth, then it seems at first sight quite acceptable from the Christian viewpoint. But our critical doubt as to its tenability is aroused when we consider that the historicistic view is a philosophical total-view of empirical reality within the temporal order of our experiential horizon. And this total view originated from the absolutization of the scientific historical viewpoint. As such, it is nothing but one of the many isms in the philosophical views of reality. It is on the same footing as the others, such as mechanism, biologism, psychologism, logicism, aestheticism, moralism, et cetera. All these isms originate from the absolutization of a specific scientific viewpoint which considers empirical reality only from one of the fundamental aspects of [84] our temporal experience. These aspects are the fundamental modes or manners of this experience. As such they are only related to the how of the latter, not to the concrete what, i.e., to concrete things, or events or particular societal relationships, which we experience in these different modes or aspects. This concrete what, e.g., the battle of Waterloo, is never to be identified with just one of its aspects. It is an individual whole, which in principle functions in all the aspects of our experience.[1]

---

1   Dooyeweerd emphasizes that the 'modes' or 'aspects' of experience are not real or concrete entities; rather, they are different ways in which we experience these concrete wholes. The modes or aspects are only disclosed in the theoretical attitude, which is an abstraction from everyday or naive experience. To explain this in terms

59

The different modes or aspects of our experiential horizon are arranged in an irreversible order and display an unbreakable mutual coherence.[1] It is only in the theoretical or scientific attitude of thought that we separate them and set them in opposition to one another. And we do so in order to delimit the different specific scientific viewpoints from which empirical reality is considered and examined. In the non-theoretical and pre-scientific attitude of thought and experience we never do this. There our attention is directed immediately to concrete things and events as individual wholes; and their different aspects are only experienced implicitly, not in the way of a theoretical logical distinction.

If, in the pre-scientific attitude of experience, we try to answer the question: "What is history?," we usually say: "That which has happened in the past." From this non-theoretical experiential attitude this answer is doubtless correct. In that situation we do not reflect on the particular historical mode, or aspect, of our experience, but we give our attention [85] exclusively to the concrete what being experienced in this way. And in that way we refer to the concrete events that have occurred in the past. But if we wish to acquire an insight into the historical viewpoint, which in principle delimits the scientific field of research in historiography, there is no use in referring to the concrete what being experienced in the historical way. Rather, at that point we are much more interested in this particular mode of experience itself, that is to say, in the historical aspect of our experience as such. If I drank a cup of coffee yesterday and smoked a cigar, these facts belong to the past today. But are these activities really historical facts, and are they of any concern to the historian? They are by themselves certainly not historical facts in a typical sense; that is, they are not facts which are typically qualified by their historical aspect, such as the battle of Waterloo, the invention of typography, or the great invasion of the Allied military forces in France during the last world-war. Nevertheless, such simple things as drinking and smoking certainly have an historical aspect. In the Middle Ages one did not drink coffee or smoke cigars. The introduction of these means of enjoyment into our Western civilization has doubtless influenced our cultural life in an historical sense.

b) Delimitation of the historical aspect

But what is the historical aspect of the facts concerned? The historians themselves, insofar as they are not interested in the epistemological

---

of Husserl's phenomenology, the concrete 'thing' is Real – outside of the mind or consciousness (which both Husserl and Dooyeweerd would describe as 'transcendence'); the modes or aspects, however, are Irreal – existing only in and for consciousness. For Husserl's discussion of this distinction, see Ideas I, Introduction (p. xx) and pp. 41-42.

1   Here, and in much of this section, Dooyeweerd is taking up again his analysis of theory in Chapter One above. For further details and explanatory notes, refer to that chapter.

problems of their branch of science, are not able to answer the question concerning the specific nature of their scientific [86] viewpoint. Their attention is only directed upon the historical facts in their historical context, i.e. upon the concrete what presenting itself within the historical aspect of our experience. It is only from this aspect that they consider their scientific material. This means that they indeed abstract this aspect from the full reality of the facts as we experience them in life. The German historian, Leopold Ranke, answered the question as to the methodology of historiography as follows: "I describe how it has truly been."[1] This answer was certainly somewhat naive, since no single science is able to examine the full empirical reality of events. Other historians have said that the scientific approach is the genetic one. The science of history then is the science of becoming, or evolution. But every empirical science has its own genetic viewpoint and consequently uses the term evolution or becoming in a different sense. Therefore, this term in itself is not defined in its meaning. It is of an analogical or multivocal character.

In determining what distinguishes the historian's genetic view-point from that of the geologist or biologist or psychologist, it is its historical character that we are looking for. Consequently, it cannot be the genetic view-point which determines the historical mode of experience. Indeed, the reverse is true. How can we explain that the meaning of the terms "evolution", "development", or "becoming" vary with the different scientific viewpoints from which empirical reality is approached? Every aspect of our experiential horizon, as a [87] fundamental manner or mode of experience, has a modal structure, in which the whole temporal order and mutual coherence of the different aspects finds its inner expression. This modal structure displays a nuclear moment, which guarantees the irreducible proper meaning of the aspect concerned. But this modal kernel can unfold this meaning only in an unbreakable context with a series of so-called analogical moments. These latter refer backward or forward, respectively, to the modal kernels of the aspects which have either an earlier or a later place in the temporal order of experience.[2] In conformity to this different direction of their reference, we distinguish the analogical moments into retrospective and anticipatory ones. Their specific meaning is always determined by the nuclear moment of the experiential aspect in which they function. From this it follows that only an exact analysis of the modal structure of the historical aspect of our experience can bring to light both the proper meaning of this experiential mode and its place in the temporal order of the aspects.

1   See, for example, Leopold von Ranke, The Secret of World History: Selected Writings on the Art and Science of History, trans. Roger Wines (Bronx, NY: Fordham University Press, 1981).

2   For further explanation of this backward and forward 'reference,' see § 14 below.

c) *The nuclear meaning of the historical aspect*

The historicist view of the temporal world could not absolutize the historical aspect of our experience without eliminating its modal structure. For it is this very structure which excludes in principle any attempt at reducing all the other modes of experience to mere modalities of the historical aspect. The proper sense of the latter can only reveal itself in an unbreakable context with that of the other aspects; and this state of affairs explains why a consistent or radical historicism [88] must lead to nihilism, which denies that there is any meaning to history. For the absolutization of a particular aspect, whose meaning is only relative, destroys this meaning and accordingly results in utter meaninglessness.

To strike Historicism in its essence, we must try to trace the modal kernel of the historical mode of experience. What is the irreducible nuclear moment of its structure? An etymological inquiry into the term "history" itself cannot help us detect it. This word is of Greek origin and had initially no other meaning than investigation. This neutral sense revealed itself also in the use of the term natural history, which acquired a particular meaning only since the advent of Romanticist philosophy and Darwinian evolutionism, which used it in a direct context with the history of mankind. It was the analogical, i.e., the multivocal concept of evolution or development, which served as a kind of a basic denominator for so-called natural history as well as for history in its proper use.

Nevertheless, even from the historicist standpoint, it was necessary to indicate a criterion for the distinction between the fields of research of historiography proper and that of the natural sciences which are concerned with the examination of natural history in its genetic sense. Now, all modern philosophical attempts at delimiting the proper historical scientific viewpoint from that of the genetic natural sciences resulted in accepting the notion of culture as the central criterion. [89]

But what was understood by culture? Here the influence of the religious basic motive of Humanistic thought which I have explained in my first lecture [chapter three] clearly manifested itself. The Italian philosopher, Vico, who was the first to set the historical mode of thought over against the mathematical and scientific one, identified culture with human society which he called the civil world. In clear opposition to the Cartesian point of view, he said that it is not nature which is created by human reason, but only the civil world of human culture.[1] Naturally, Descartes had not pretended that properly speaking nature is created by human thought. It was only the mathematical and mechanistic picture of nature which was viewed as an autonomous creation of methodical mathematical thought. Vico, however, set himself against this mechanistic world-picture from the standpoint of the Humanist freedom-motive.

---

1 Vico, op. cit.

According to him, the true creative freedom of human reason does not reveal itself in mathematical and natural scientific thought, but in the creation of the cultural world of human society. And this creation occurs in an historical process by the rational mind of the nations. Human culture, as a result of this creative process, embraces all that in human social life surpasses the animal level of existence: the social institutions of marriage and family, political institutions, the forms of conventional social intercourse, language, economy, fine arts, law, morality, religion. In this way, culture was viewed as a second world in addition to the world of nature, a world of a specific historical [90] reality. And the principles of its social order were supposed to be found in practical human reason as the creator of this civil world.

This identification of culture with [i.e. Holding culture to be identical to – ed. DFMS] the whole of man's societal world maintained itself in all the later philosophical theories of history. It was the very basis of the historicist world-view which originated in an absolutization of the historical aspect of human experience. Every ism in the realm of philosophical world-views begins with the identification of one particular aspect or mode of experience with the whole reality of our empirical world. In this way a truly critical analysis of the notion of culture was excluded in principle in the case of the historicist world-view as well. A reality of a purely cultural character cannot exist. It is the noun-form of the word culture which favored this misconception, just as the noun-form of the term life favored the identification of reality with the biological mode of experience, which in turn led to the vitalistic, or biologistic world-view. We shall, therefore, replace the noun culture with the adjective cultural, in order to emphasize that it is only one modal aspect of our temporal world which is meant. Taken in this modal sense, the term "cultural" means nothing but a particular (experiential) mode of formation, or molding, which is fundamentally different from all modes of formation found in nature and conceived in the physico-chemical or biotic aspects of experience. It is a controlling mode whereby form is given to a material according to a freely elaborate and variable plan. [91]

A spider spins its web with faultless precision; but it does so after a fixed and uniform pattern prescribed by the instinct of the species. It lacks free control or dominion over its material, which is the very condition of the variability of all cultural formation. Thus the cultural mode of formation must receive its specific qualification through freedom of control, domination or power. This is why the great cultural commandment given to man at creation reads: "Subdue the earth and have dominion over it" (Genesis 1:28). And if the genuine historical viewpoint of historiography is that of the cultural development of humanity, it follows that formative power or control must also be the modal kernel of the historical aspect. It is this nuclear moment which alone can give the analogical or multi-vocal concept of development its proper historical sense. The historical development of mankind means in principle, then, the development of its formative power over the world and over its societal life.

The cultural mode of formation reveals itself in two directions, which are closely connected with each other. On the one hand it is a formative power over persons, unfolding itself by giving cultural form to their societal experience; on the other hand, it appears as a controlling manner of shaping natural materials, things, or forces to cultural ends. Thus the Germans speak of Personkultur and Sachkultur. Since all cultural phenomena are bound to human society in its historical development, the development of Sachkultur is in principle dependent on that of [92] Personkultur. For the cultural formation of natural materials or forces can only come about through human beings who must learn it by socio-cultural education, given in a socio-cultural form to their minds. In addition, both Personkultur and Sachkultur presuppose the leading ideas for projects, which leading figures or groups in history seek to realize in a human society. Therefore, the formative power of these leading figures and groups always implies an intentional relation to such ideas.

These ideas cannot be realized according to the merely subjective conception of those who propagate them. They must assume a socio-cultural form so that they themselves may be able to exercise formative power in the relationships of society. By way of example, I refer to the cultural influence of the ideas of natural law, especially the idea of the innate human rights, or to the cultural influence of the technological ideas of great inventors, the aesthetic ideas of great artists, the moral ideas of the preachers of new moralities, et cetera. Such ideas are not of a cultural historical significance in themselves, but they acquire a historical significance as soon as they begin to exercise formative power in human society. They can be realized only in typical total structures of societal relationships which in principle function in all aspects of our experiential horizon, such as a state, an industrial community, a school, a religious community, and so forth. The empirical reality of human social life can, therefore, never be exhausted in its cultural-historical aspect, as Historicism assumed. All that is [93] real or that really happens in human society is more than merely historical.

§ 14. Anticipations and retrocipations in the notion of 'development'

After having established in this way the nuclear moment of the historical aspect of our experience, we may now turn to the analogical concept of historical development. In the previous lecture we observed that the Historical School, which in the first half of the last century introduced the new historical mode of thought into all branches of social scientific research, sharply emphasized this concept of historical developement. And it is beyond doubt that it is this very notion which enables the historian to discover inner coherences in the temporal succession of historical facts and changes. It is the process of historical development which binds the present historical condition of human society to the previous phases of its history. If this notion of development were to be abandoned, no single synthetic insight into a historical process would be possible, and historiography would degenerate into a collection of assorted reports from the past.

But it is exactly the analogical or multivocal character of this concept which has raised serious doubt as to its scientific significance. The famous Dutch historian, Huizinga, has asked the question whether our speaking of development in history does not rest on a mere metaphor. This word "development," he says, is taken from biology, where it relates to the process of evolution of a living organism. But what meaning can it have when it is transferred to history?[1] Our answer must be that, as a biotic analogy in our cultural historical mode of experience, the notion of historical development is [94] implied in that of socio-cultural life, which can certainly not be a mere metaphor. It is true that all other modes of life, such as the sensitive, cultural, economic, aesthetic, juridical, moral and the faith aspects of life, refer back to the original mode of organic life which is their indispensable foundation. But this does not mean that they could be reduced to the latter, or, if this turns out to be impossible, that they might be considered mere metaphors on the same footing as for instance the metaphorical use of the term "play" in the phrase: "The play of the waves." The sense of life and development is not exhausted in that of their biological mode of manifestation. Jesus Christ has said that man shall not live by bread alone, but by every word that proceeds out of the mouth of God. Here the term "live" is certainly not used metaphorically, but much rather in the religious fullness of its meaning. So we must try to discover the particular meaning of historical development from the modal structure of the cultural-historical aspect of experience.

We have seen that the proper meaning of a particular aspect of our experience can only reveal itself in its unbreakable coherence with that of all the other modal aspects. And this coherence of meaning finds expression in a series of analogical moments in its structure referring backwards and forwards respectively to all aspects which have an earlier or later place in the temporal order.[2] This means that every analogical moment in the cultural or historical mode of experience has

---

1 See, for example, Johan Huizinga, Men and Ideas: History, the Middle Ages, the Renaissance, trans. J.S. Holmes and Hans van Marle (New York: Meridian, 1959), pp. 17-76.

2 For Dooyeweerd, the multiplicity of modal aspects (outlined above at § 2 [a]) cohere in an irreversible order, proceeding from lower modes – numerical, spatial, etc. – to

its particular place in the order of analogies and cannot reveal its proper cultural historical sense apart from the others.[1] [95] As a biotic analogy in the cultural sense of history, cultural development refers backwards to development in its biological sense, but not directly. The historical mode of experience is immediately founded in the logical or analytical mode of distinguishing our experiences. In other words, the cultural-historical aspect is directly founded in the logical. Without the basis of logical distinction, no single historical experience is possible.

Let us take for example the battle of Waterloo as a historical fact. The famous Austrian economist, Hayek, raised the question whether the work of the farmers, who tried desperately to save their crops on the battle-fields, also belonged to the battle.[2] This question is very instructive, for it proves that our historical mode of experiencing the battle of Waterloo cannot be founded on a record of sensory perception alone. From the sensory viewpoint, the work of the farmers took place without a doubt on the battlefield. But implicitly, we make an analytical, or logical distinction, between the actions of persons, whether or not they pertain to the battle as a historical contest of power between Napoleon's forces and those of his allied opponents.

This inner coherence between the logical and the historical aspects finds expression in their respective modal structures. The historical aspect must therefore display logical analogies. I shall restrict myself to indicating that particular logical analogy in the historical mode of experience which gives a further determination to the analogical concept of historical development. In the logical aspect [96] of our thought and experience, we encounter the fundamental logical relation of contradiction. We experience a logical contradiction when an argument avails itself of two propositions which exclude one another in a logical sense. In this case we posit that this mode of reasoning is illogical; and this statement implies a normative evaluation, since it implies the validity of a fundamental logical norm of thought which forbids such contradictions.

Now it is indisputable that in all experiential aspects which are based on the logical,[3] an analogy of this normative logical contrast is found. This is a strong indication of the normative character of these aspects,

---

higher order modes – the jural, moral, pistic. The lower modes "found" the higher ones, and the higher aspects "open" the lower aspects (thus in what follows he notes that the historical aspect is 'founded' in the logical aspect). What he emphasizes here is that within each aspect, analogies are referring to all of the other aspects because of their "unbreakable coherence." Analogies which point to 'higher' aspects are "anticipations;" analogies which refer to 'lower' modes are "retrocipations."

1 Historicism, Dooyeweerd is arguing, fails to honor the coherence of the aspects of reality by divorcing the historical from the other aspects to which it refers.

2 Hayek, "The Facts of the Social Sciences," Ethics 54 (1943), pp. 1-13.

3 'Lower' aspects such as the numerical or spatial modes are not 'based' or 'founded' on the logical – only those that are 'higher' in the order of coherence, such as the social or economic aspects.

which means that within their modes of experience, behavior is not subject to laws of nature, but to norms, relating to what ought to be. I refer to the contrasts: polite-impolite, decent-indecent, and other such contrasts which function in the aspect of conventional social intercourse; to the contrast: linguistically right or wrong, which we meet with in the linguistic aspect of experience; to the contrasts: aesthetic-unaesthetic, economic-uneconomic, lawful-unlawful, moral-immoral, believing-unbelieving, which occur respectively in the aesthetic, economic, juridical, moral and faith aspects of our experiential horizon.

Hence, the analogical notion of historical development is unbreakably connected with the contrast of historical-unhistorical, or progressive-reactionary. By this contrast we mean that the behavior or program of a leading figure or group is in line with, or contrary [97] to the requirements of historical development. As a clear analogy of the logical relation of contradiction, this contrast implies a normative criterion, so that the concept of historical development must itself have a normative cultural meaning. And since the contrast concerned appeared to be founded in the modal structure of the historical aspect itself, its normative sense cannot be reduced to a merely subjective evaluation of the factual course of history. Rather, it must be founded on an objective norm of historical development which implicitly lies at the foundation of the cultural-historical mode of experience. No person whose historical consciousness has not been supplanted by non-historical political considerations will deny that from a politico-historical viewpoint the so-called counter-revolutionary movement in Europe, which after the defeat of Napoleon strove for the restoration of the medieval feudal regime, was of a reactionary character. This judgment will be independent of the question of whether or not one admires the cultural forms of medieval society, and whether or not the memory of those times is recalled with a kind of romantic desire.

§ 15. The normative criterion for determining 'development': differentiation

a) The unfolding process

But on what objective norm of historical development may this judgment be founded? The German historical school made a sharp distinction between living and dead elements in the historical tradition of a nation. The former should be utilized in the progressive line of further development, the latter should be sloughed off. This was the reason that the Historical school rejected any reactionary [98] attempt to revive the medieval politic régime. But this school failed to produce a supra-arbitrary norm of cultural development whereby we can establish what constitutes the proper historical meaning of the terms progress and reaction. And the reason why it failed is that its conception of historical development clung exclusively to the biotic analogies in the cultural-historical mode of experience. Taking the natural development of a living organism as a pattern, the adherents of this school stressed the organic character of the historical process of development. The continuity of this development, they pointed out, binds the present and future condition of a national civilization to its historical past. The distinction between living and dead elements in the historical tradition of a people was also exclusively oriented by them to biotic analogies in the process of cultural development.

But these analogies are of a retrospective character. They refer backward in the order of time to an earlier aspect of our experience which lacks a normative character.[1] Development in its biological sense is not ruled by norms, i. e., by rules relating to what ought to be, but by laws of nature. In the biotic aspect of time, the development of a multicellular living organism displays only the natural phases of birth, ripening adolescence, age and decline. But in the historical process of cultural development a normative human vocation reveals itself, a cultural task committed to man at his creation. This task cannot be fulfilled [99] except in the anticipatory, or prospective direction of time in which the historico-cultural aspect of our temporal world opens up its sense by unfolding its anticipatory moments. It will be recalled that anticipatory moments in the structure of an experiential aspect are those analogical moments which refer forward to aspects occupying a later place in the temporal order of our experience. We have established that all the aspects which in this order are founded on the logical mode of experience, inclusive of the historical aspect, are of a normative character. Therefore, the nuclear moment of the historico-cultural mode of development – namely, formative power – has itself a normative sense, since it implies a normative cultural vocation and task, committed to man at creation. Even the most terrible misuse of cultural power in our sinful world cannot make power itself sinful, nor can it detract from the normative sense of man's cultural vocation.

Until the cultural-historical aspect of a human society discloses the anticipatory moments of its meaning, it shows itself to be in a rigid and primitive condition. Primitive cultures are enclosed in undifferentiated organized communities, which display a strong tendency towards isola-

---

1   The 'organic' or 'biotic' aspect to which this notion of development refers precedes the logical aspect; therefore, it lacks a sense of normativity required for locating normative criteria for determining what constitutes 'development.'

tion.[1] As long as such primitive societies maintain their isolation in history, there can be no question of cultural development in the sense in which it is understood in historiography proper. They display a totalitarian character since they embrace their members every sphere of their [100] personal lives and also because the temporal existence of the individual is completely dependent on membership of the family or sib, respectively, and on that of the tribal community. There is no room as yet for a differentiation of culture in the particular spheres of formative power – those, namely, of science, fine arts, commerce and industry, of state and church, and so forth. Since such undifferentiated communities fulfill all the tasks for which, on a higher level of civilization, particular organizations are formed, there is only one single undifferentiated cultural sphere. A rigid tradition, often deified by a pagan belief, and anxiously guarded by the leaders of the group, has the monopoly of formative power. The development process by which such cultural communities are formed shows only analogies of the biotic phases of birth, ripening, adolescence, age and decline. The duration of their existence is dependent on that of the popular and tribal communities by which they are sustained. They may vanish from the scene without leaving any trace in the history of mankind. This is how radical historicism conceived the course of every civilization and thus Spengler predicted the inescapable decline of Western culture.

But the situation is quite different in the historical development of cultures that are opened up. From the ancient cultural centers of world-history – such as Babylon, Egypt, Palestine, Crete, Greece, Rome, Byzantium – essential tendencies of development passed over into medieval and modern Western civilization. They fertilized the Germanic and Arabian [101] cultures and this fertilization gave rise to new forms of civilization. This opened-up cultural development has been freed from rigid dependence upon the living conditions of small popular or tribal communities. It does not move within the narrow boundaries of a closed and undifferentiated cultural group. But, like a fertilizing stream, it is always seeking new channels along which to continue its course.

The process by which the cultural aspect of a society is opened up always occurs in a conflict between the guardians of tradition and the propounders of new ideas. The formative power of tradition is enormous, for, in a concentrated form, it embodies cultural treasures amassed in the course of centuries. Every generation is historically bound to former

---

1   In the process of historical development or unfolding, the diverse social 'spheres' (such as state, family, church, club, etc.) become differentiated as distinct spheres, each with their own realm of sovereignty. In primitive cultures, Dooyeweerd suggests, these spheres remain undifferentiated and thus tend toward totalitarian control. In this sense, even medieval Europe would be a 'primitive' or 'undifferentiated' culture.

generations by its tradition. We are all dominated by it to a much higher degree than we realize. In a primitive closed civilization, its power is nearly absolute; in an opened-up culture, tradition is no longer unassailable, but it has the indispensable role of guarding that measure of continuity in cultural progress without which cultural life would be impossible. In the struggle with the power of tradition, the progressive ideas of so-called molders of history have themselves to be purged of their revolutionary subjectivity and adjusted to the norm of historical continuity. Even Jacob Burckhardt, that great disciple of Leopold von Ranke, although strongly affected by the historicist relativism, held to the norm of continuity as a last guarantee against the decline of all civilization.[1] [102]

The opening-up process of cultural life is characterized by the destruction of the undifferentiated and exclusive power of primitive communities. It is a process of cultural differentiation which is balanced by an increasing cultural integration. It is effected by the bursting of the rigid walls of isolation which had enclosed primitive cultural life. This is achieved by submitting the latter to fruitful contact with civilizations which have already burst the bonds of tradition, having been previously opened up to outside influences.

Since August Comte and Herbert Spencer, the criterion of differentiation and integration has been accepted by many sociologists to distinguish more highly developed societies from primitive ones. The process of differentiation was viewed as a consequence of the division of labor, and an attempt was made to explain it in a natural scientific manner in analogy to the increasing differentiation of organic life in the higher developed organisms. But I do not understand the term "cultural differentiation" in this pseudo-natural scientific sense; much rather I have in mind a differentiation in the typical structures of the different social relationships presenting themselves in a human society. A primitive sib or clan displays mixed traits of an extended family, a business organization, a club or school, a state, a religious community, and so forth. In a differentiated society, on the other hand, all these communities are sharply distinguished from one another, so that each of them can reveal its proper inner nature, notwithstanding [103] the fact that there are all kinds of interrelations between them. Each of these differentiated communities has its own typical historico-cultural sphere of formative power, whose inner boundaries are determined by the inner nature of the communities to which they belong.

---

1 See, for example, Jacob Burckhardt, On History and Historians, trans. Harry Zohn (New York: Harper & Row, 1965).

b) *Individuality-structures*

The typical structures of these communities are really structures of individuality, since they are typical structures of an individual societal
whole.[1] With the exception of natural communities such as marriage
and family, which have a typical biotical foundation, they are all typically founded in historico-cultural power formations, which presuppose
the process of cultural differentiation and integration. Consequently, although they cannot be realized before this historical process has started,
their typical structures cannot be more variable than the modal structures of their different aspects, since these structural norms determine
the inner nature of the differentiated communities. As such, they must
be founded in the order of creation, which has determined the inner nature of all that presents itself within our temporal world. And they are
not to be traced in a natural scientific way since they are structural
norms which may be violated by man.

In the temporal world-order, norms are only given as principles which
need a formation by man in accordance with the level of historical development of a society. The societal forms which they assume in this
way are consequently of a variable character; but the structural principles, to which [104] these forms give a variable positive content, are not
variable historical phenomena since they alone make all variable formations of the societal communities possible. Neither the inner nature of
marriage, nor that of the family, the state, the church, an industrial community, and the like, are variable in time, but only the social forms in
which they are realized. The Historical school did stress the absolute individuality of any national community but it overlooked the typical
structures of individuality which determine the inner nature of the different communities, including the national one, which as such cannot be
of a merely historical character. Nevertheless, it is true that the process
of cultural differentiation and integration is at the same time a process
of growing individualization of human cultural life; for it is only in an
opened-up and differentiated civilization that individuality assumes a
really historical significance. It is true that in primitive, closed cultural
areas individuality is not altogether lacking. But in consequence of the
rigid dominance of tradition, the individuality retains a certain traditional uniformity so that from generation to generation such closed cultures display generally speaking the same, individual features. It is for
this reason that historiography in its proper sense takes no interest in
these cultural individualities.

As soon, however, as the process of differentiation and integration
commences, the historical task of individual cultural dispositions and
talents becomes [105] manifest. Every individual contribution to the

---

1   The notion of "individuality-structures" is the focus of Volume 3 of *A New Critique
    of Theoretical Thought: The Structures of Individuality of Temporal Reality*.

opening up of the cultural aspect of human society becomes in the course of time a contribution to the cultural development of mankind, which has a worldwide perspective. Accordingly, the individuality of cultural leaders and groups assumes a deepened historical sense. It is the opening-up process of human culture also which alone can give rise to national communities. A nation, viewed as a socio-cultural unit, should be sharply distinguished from the primitive ethnic unit, which is called a popular or tribal community. A real national cultural whole is not a natural product of blood and soil, but the result of a process of differentiation and integration in the cultural formation of human society. In a national community, all ethnic differences between the various groups of a population are integrated into a new individual whole, which lacks the undifferentiated totalitarian traits of a closed and primitive ethnic unit as a tribe or folkship. The different peoples of the United States of America are doubtless united in a national community, but how different are the ethnic components which are integrated into this national whole.

It was, therefore, unmistakable proof of the reactionary character of the myth of blood and soil propagated by German Nazism when it tried to undermine the national consciousness of the Germanic peoples by reviving the primitive ethnic idea of Volkstum. Similarly, it is unmistakable proof of the retrograde tendency of all modern totalitarian [106] political systems when they attempt to annihilate the process of cultural differentiation and individualization by a methodical mental equalization (Gleichschaltung) of all cultural spheres; for this equalization implies a fundamental denial of the value of the individual personality in the unfolding (opening-up) process of history.

So we may posit that the norm of cultural differentiation, integration and individualization is really an objective norm of the historical unfolding process of human society. It is founded in the divine world order, since it indicates the necessary conditions of this prospective unfolding process, without which mankind cannot fulfill its historical task committed to it by the great cultural commandment. Furthermore, it provides us with an objective criterion to distinguish truly progressive from reactionary tendencies in history. The unfolding or opening-up process of the cultural-historical aspect occurs in the anticipatory or prospective direction of the temporal order. It must, therefore, be possible to point to the anticipatory moments in its modal structure by which the inner coherence of meaning of the historical process of development with that of the subsequently arranged normative aspects of our temporal horizon of experience reveals itself. Historicism is not able to do that, since it has reduced these normative aspects to mere modalities of the historical process of development. Consequently, it negates their irreducible character and meaning. [107] To begin with, the progressive unfolding process of history is characterized by the disclosure of a symbolic, or linguistic anticipation in the historical mode of experience. The linguistic aspect of our experiential horizon is that of communication by a medium of signs which have a symbolical meaning. These signs may be words or other symbols. They play an essential role in our social experience. In the opening-up process of historical development, that which really has an historical significance begins to separate itself from what is historically insignificant. This gives rise to a symbolical signification of historical facts in order to preserve the memory of them.

Hegel and von Ranke held that history proper did not start before the need arose to preserve the memory of historical events by means of chronicles, records and other means. The so-called Kulturkreislehre in ethnology – which seeks to trace genetic continuity in the cultural evolution of mankind from the so-called primeval cultures of pre-history to civilizations at the highest level of development of civilization – has denied that the presence of memorials can be of any essential importance for the delimitation of this historical field of research. As its founder, Frobenius, has said, "History is action, and in comparison with this, how unessential is its symbolical recording."[1] The truth is, however, that the rise of such memorials is an unquestionable criterion of the cultural unfolding of a society in a progressive sense. Consequently, depreciating the rise of historical memorials with respect to their significance for the historical development [108] of mankind testifies to a lack of insight into the modal structure of the historical aspect of experience in its opening-up process. The fact that historical memorials, or at least, reliable oral historical information is lacking in primitive society – and only mythological representations of the genesis and development of their cultural life are found – cannot be unessential. The relatively uniform course of primitive society's process of development has not yet given the Muse of history any material worth recording as memorable in a really historical sense. An as yet closed historical consciousness clings to the biotic analogies in cultural development and inclines to a mythological interpretation of its course under the influence of a primitive religion of organic life. The disclosure of the symbolic or linguistic anticipation in the unfolding process of the historical aspect of experience is indissolubly linked to a disclosure of cultural intercourse between different nations caught up in the stream of world history. Cultural intercourse between different nations in this international sense is an anticipatory moment in the process of historical development referring forwards to the opening up of the modal aspect of conventional social intercourse.

Since the process of cultural differentiation leads to an increasing typical diversity of cultural spheres, there is a constant danger that one of

---

1   Leo Frobenius, Ursprung der Afrikanischen Kultur (1898).

these spheres may try to expand its formative power in an excessive manner at the expense of the others. Indeed, since the dissolution of the ecclesiastically unified culture which [109] prevailed in medieval European civilization, there has been a running battle between the emancipated cultural spheres of the state, of natural science, of industry and commerce, and so forth, to acquire the supremacy one over the other. In the progressive unfolding process of history, therefore, the preservation of a harmonious relationship between the differentiated cultural spheres becomes of vital interest to all of human society. But this cultural harmony can be guaranteed only if the process of historical development complies with the normative principle of cultural economy. This principle forbids any excessive expansion of the formative power of a particular cultural sphere at the expense of the others.[1] Here the aesthetic and economic anticipations in the historical mode of experience reveal themselves in their unbreakable mutual coherence. Both principles, that of cultural economy and that of cultural harmony, appeal to the inner nature of the differentiated cultural spheres as determined by the typical structures of individuality of the spheres of society to which they belong. Thus they, too, are well founded in the divine world-order. In the unfolding (opening-up) process of human culture, as soon as the natural bounds of the different cultural spheres are ignored through an excessive expansion of one of them, disastrous tensions and conflicts arise in human society. This may evoke convulsive reactions on the part of those cultural spheres which are threatened, or it may even lead to the complete ruin of a civilization, unless counter-tendencies in the process of development [110] manifest themselves before it is too late and acquire sufficient cultural power to check the excess expansion of power of a particular cultural factor.

It is in such consequences of the violation of the principles of cultural economy and harmony in the historical unfolding-process that the juridical anticipation in history comes to light. At this point we find ourselves confronted with the Hegelian adage: "Die Weltgeschichte ist der Weltgericht."[2] I do not accept this dictum in the sense in which Hegel meant it, but rather in the sense that the violation of the normative principles to which the unfolding process of the cultural historical aspect of human society is subject is avenged in the course of world-history. This may be verified by observing the consequences of such violations.

---

1   In other words, each sphere is sovereign within its realm of 'jurisdiction.' The state, for instance, cannot impinge on the sphere of the church.

2   "The history of the world is the judgement of the world." G.W.F. Hegel, Philosophy of Right, trans. T.M. Knox (Oxford: Clarendon Press, 1962), § 340. Hegel draws this from Schiller.

§ 16. Faith and culture

When, finally, the question is asked concerning the fundamental cause of disharmony in the unfolding process of history, we come face to face with the problem concerning the relationship between faith and culture and with the religious basic motives which operate in the central sphere of human life. The disharmony I am referring to belongs, alas, to the progressive line of cultural development, since it can only reveal itself in the historical unfolding process of cultural differentiation. The conflicts and tensions which are particularly to be observed in modern Western civilization, cannot occur in a primitive, closed culture. Since any expansion of the formative power of mankind over the world gives rise to an increasing manifestation of [111] human sin, the historical opening-up process is marked by blood and tears. It does not lead to an earthly paradise.

What, then, is the sense in all this extreme endeavor, conflict, and misery to which man submits in order to fulfill his cultural task in the world? Radical Historicism, as it manifested itself in all its consequences in Spengler's Decline of the West, deprived the history of mankind of any hope for the future and made it meaningless. This is the result of the absolutization of the historical aspect of experience; for we have seen that the latter can only reveal its meaning in an unbreakable coherence with all the other aspects of our temporal experiential horizon. This temporal horizon itself refers to the human ego as its central point of reference, both in its spiritual communion with all other human egos and in its central relationship to the Divine Author of all that has been created. Ultimately, the problem of the meaning of history revolves around the question: "Who is man himself and what is his origin and his final destination?" Outside of the central biblical revelation of creation, the fall into sin and redemption through Jesus Christ, no real answer is to be found to this question. The conflicts and dialectical tensions which occur in the process of the opening-up process of human cultural life result from the absolutization of what is relative. And every absolutization takes its origin from the spirit of apostasy, from the spirit of the civitas terrena, the kingdom of darkness, as Augustine called it.[1]

There would be no future hope for mankind and [112] for the whole process of man's cultural development if Jesus Christ had not become the spiritual center and his kingdom the ultimate end of world-history. This center and end of world-history is bound neither to the Western nor to any other civilization. But it will lead the new mankind as a whole to

---

1   Augustine, The City of God, trans. Henry Bettenson (London: Penguin, 1984), XIV.28.

its true destination since it has conquered the world by the divine love revealed in its self-sacrifice.[1]

---

1   1 John 5:19f.; Augustine, City of God, X.6.

PART THREE

Philosophy and Theology

Chapter Five

Philosophy, Theology, and Religion

§ 17. The relation between philosophy and theology: a historical survey

It may seem a dangerous enterprise for a non-theologian to speak concerning the relation between philosophy and theology. Nevertheless, as representative of a philosophical trend which claims to have a radical Christian starting-point, I have been obliged to do so; especially since I am of the opinion that this Christian philosophy does not derive its fundamentals from theology in its scientific sense, and, therefore, should be sharply distinguished from the latter.

It is not surprising that many theologians are nonplussed by this point of view. And this initial doubt may easily change into suspicion when this new philosophy subjects the traditional philosophical fundamentals of dogmatic theological thought to a radical criticism and requires an inner reformation of these fundamentals from the biblical viewpoint. Such suspicion is understandable, since philosophy has been a dangerous rival to Christian theology from the very outset. Ever since the Greek thinker, Parmenides, the founder of Western metaphysics, philosophical theory has been opposed to popular belief. It presented itself as the pathway of truth over against that of doxa (deceitful opinion), bound by [114] sensory representations and emotions.[1] In Plato's famous dialogue, Phaedo, Socrates says that it is only destined to the philosophers to approach the race of the gods. It was the common conviction of all Greek thinkers, who held to the possibility of theological knowledge, that true theology can only be of a philosophical character and cannot be founded on faith, but on theoretic thought only. It is true that Plato did not reject the possibility of a divine revelation, received in a state of holy enthusiasm, but he denied that such revelations could be in any sense the source of real theological knowledge.

---

1 "Meet it is that thou shouldst learn all things, as well the unshaken heart of well-rounded truth, as the opinions of mortals in which is no true belief at all," Fr. 342 (Kirk and Raven, p. 267).

a) The Augustinian tradition

It is, therefore, completely understandable that the Church Fathers in their treatises on Christian doctrine emphasized that Christian theology has its own principle of knowledge, namely, the Word-revelation.[1] And because it possesses this principle (which contains the absolute truth), Christian theology surpasses, in their opinion, all pagan philosophy in its certainty of knowledge. Theoretic thought cannot achieve truth, unless it is enlightened by this principle. Therefore, they held, pagan philosophy is full of errors and cannot be accepted as an autonomous science.[2] Christian theology, they believed, is itself the supreme science, the true Christian philosophy. Greek and Graeco-Roman philosophy, at their very best, can render some services to the sacra doctrina – provided, however, that they remain servants, subject to the control of theology.

It was especially Augustine who defended this view of the relation between philosophy and Christian theology. His rejection of [115] the autonomy of philosophical thought is quite in accordance with the position of the new Christian philosophy which I had in mind at the outset of this lecture. But his view of the relation between Christian theology and philosophy suffers from an ambiguous use of the term theology.[3] On the one hand, this word is used in the sense of the true knowledge of God and ourselves, and it refers to the holy doctrine of the Church. As such it cannot have a theoretical, scientific meaning, as will become evident presently. On the other hand, Christian theology refers to a theoretical explanation of the articles of faith in their scientific confrontation with the texts of Holy Writ and with heretical views. In this sense, Christian theology is bound to theoretical human thought which cannot claim the infallibility of God's Word. It was the influence of Greek philosophy which led to the fatal step of confusing theoretical Christian theology with the true knowledge of God and true self-knowledge

---

1   For Dooyeweerd the "Word-revelation" is more encompassing than the Bible as the inscripturated Word of God. The Bible points at God's self-revelation in creation and Incarnation. The Bible is the fundamental special revelation, communicated to the "heart," which serves to 'interpret' the Divine world-order. For a discussion, see Olthuis, "Dooyeweerd on Religion and Faith," pp. 24-25, 32-38.

2   Cp. Augustine, De Doctrina Christiana, II.xxxix.58-xlii.63.

3   Dooyeweerd's relation to Augustine is one of both debt and distance: on the one hand, Dooyeweerd sees in Augustine a precursor to the Christian philosophy he is developing, insofar as Augustine recognized that knowledge begins from and is grounded in supratheoretical commitments (credum ut intelligam). But Dooyeweerd feels that Augustine failed to properly distinguish theology and a Christian philosophy as two distinct disciplines, precisely because he lacked a precise definition of theology. Sometimes, by 'theology,' Augustine refers to what Dooyeweerd would describe as 'religion;' but at other times, he defines theology as a theoretical science concerned with a specific aspect. Dooyeweerd will carefully distinguish these two senses with different terms.

(Deum et animam scire). The theological gnosis, permeated by Greek philosophical ideas, was elevated above the simple belief of the congregation. The whole conception of the so-called 'sacred theology' as the regina scientiarum [queen of the sciences] was of Greek origin. In the third book of his Metaphysics, chapter two, Aristotle says that the metaphysical doctrine of the ultimate goal and of the good has the control and guidance over all other sciences, which, as its slaves, are not even allowed to contradict its truths.[1] This statement clearly refers to the metaphysical knowledge of God, which in the second chapter of the first book was [116] called the "guiding and most estimable science." Consequently philosophical theology was considered the Queen of all sciences. This thesis of Aristotle was then applied to Christian theology in its theoretical, dogmatical sense. And this theology in turn was denominated as Christian philosophy. This meant that philosophical problems were merely discussed in a theological context.

In the 9th Century, John Scotus Erigena defended the thesis that true philosophy is identical with true religion. In his treatise on predestination, he appealed to Augustine's treatise on true religion to corroborate this view.[2] And in line with Augustine he identified Christian philosophy with dogmatical theology as the theoretical explanation of the canons of the Christian religion. "What else is true philosophy, than the explanation of the rules of true religion?" This identification of dogmatical theology with Christian philosophy on the one hand, and, with the Christian religion as expressed in the holy doctrine of the Church, on the other, remained characteristic of the Augustinian tradition in Scholasticism.

b) The Thomistic tradition

The Summa Theologiae of Thomas Aquinas, which introduced a new view, displays the same fundamental ambiguity in the use of the terms "theology" and "sacra doctrina." This prodigious work starts with a discussion of the question as to whether sacra doctrina is necessary ad humanam salutem [for human salvation] and whether it is a science. These questions are answered in the affirmative.[3] It is necessary ad humanam salutem that there be a [117] doctrine according to the divine revelation in addition to the philosophical sciences, which are studied by the light of the natural human reason alone. And it is science of a higher rank than philosophy since its principle of knowledge is of a su-

---

1 Metaphysics, III.2; VI; XII.
2 Augustine, Of True Religion, in Augustine, Earlier Writings, trans. J.H.S. Burleigh (Philadelphia: Westminster, 1953), v.8: "So it is taught and believed as a chief point in man's salvation that philosophy, i.e., the pursuit of wisdom, cannot be quite divorced from religion."
3 Summa Theologiae, Ia.1.1.

pra-natural character.[1] As such it does not need the necessary aid of the philosophical sciences, though it can use them as its slaves to facilitate the understanding of its supranatural truths. This is justified by the insufficiency of the human intellect which cannot understand the supra-natural truths of the holy doctrine without the basis of the natural truths which are known by reason alone.

These explanations have puzzled the commentators of the Summa not a little. What was meant by "sacra doctrina"? Thomas even identified it with Holy Scripture: "Sacra Scriptura seu doctrina," as he wrote in his discussions on the scientific character of the holy doctrine.[2] Some commentators were of the opinion that by sacra doctrina the Christian faith was meant. Others interpreted it as theology in its proper, scientific sense. Again others ascribed to it the sense of the holy doctrine of the church viewed apart from theology and faith. Pope Leo XIII put an end to this uncertainty in his Encyclical Aeterni Patris in which he emphatically established that theology needs philosophy to give it the character and spirit of a science.

In any case, Thomas' view of the relation between Christian theology and philosophy differs in principle from that of Augustine. Thomas no longer identifies [117] dogmatical theology and Christian philosophy with each other. The question of a Christian philosophy no longer exists.[3] Philosophy is accepted as an autonomous science including a philosophical or natural theology which refers to the natural light of reason alone. The Thomistic philosophy is the Aristotelian system, at some points elaborated in an original way and mixed with Augustinian, Neo-platonic and Stoic ideas. Christian theology, on the other hand, is elevated to the rank of a supra-natural science surpassing philosophy both in dignity and in certainty of knowledge, due to its infallible, supra-natural principles originating in divine revelation. Since the natural truths of philosophy cannot contradict the supra-natural verities of holy Christian doctrine, the Aristotelian philosophy is accommodated to the latter, as far as appearances are concerned. Nevertheless, philosophy itself is withdrawn from the internal control of the Word of God. And the supra-natural character of Christian theology is justified by the fact that it must take its knowledge from divine revelation. But the very problem concerning the scientific character of this knowledge is masked by the ambiguous use of the term sacra doctrina. This led Thomas to a fatal

---

1   ST, Ia.1.5.

2   ST, Ia.1.2-3.

3   For a delineation of the impact of Aquinas' disjunction on the history of philosophy, taking up Dooyeweerd's analysis, see James K.A. Smith, "The Art of Christian Atheism: Faith and Philosophy in Early Heidegger," Faith and Philosophy 14 (1997): 71-81.

identification of theology with the Holy Scriptures, on the one hand, and with the doctrine of the Church, on the other.

c) Barth

The lack of a sharp distinction between the Word-revelation as the central principle of knowledge and the proper scientific object of dogmatic theology has persisted in the later discussions concerning [119] the relation between dogmatic theology and philosophy, both in Roman Catholic and in Protestant circles. For the moment I shall restrict myself to the view developed by Karl Barth in the first volume of his Kirchliche Dogmatik since it is representative of an influential trend in contemporary Reformed theology.

On the one hand, Barth contrasts dogmatic theology and philosophy in a radical way. The former is instrumental in finding true knowledge of God in Jesus Christ. The principle of theological knowledge is the Word of God, and this Word is a consuming fire for all philosophy. For philosophy can only originate from autonomous human thought which is corrupted by sin. A Christian philosophy is a contradictio in terminus.[1] This is why Barth, in sharp opposition to the view of Dr. Abraham Kuyper, even denies that the epistemology of theology is of a philosophical character. Dogmatic theology, as an instrument of God's Word, must elaborate its own epistemology without interference from philosophy, Barth maintains.[2]

On the other hand, Barth is obliged to admit that dogmatical theology, as a science, does not have another intellectual tool at its disposal than that of which philosophy also avails itself, namely, theoretical thought, even though it is thoroughly inadequate for true theological thought. This [lack of an alternative to theoretical thought] is the reason that the theologian cannot escape from philosophical notions. He may take them from all kinds of systems, provided that he does not bind himself to any one of them and employs these notions only in a purely formal sense by detaching them from their material philosophical contents.[3] Ignoring for the moment this very problematical distinction between a formal and a material use of philosophical concepts, we observe that Barth, too, employs the term "theology" in an ambiguous way. On the one hand, he understands by it the true knowledge of God in Jesus Christ; on the other, dogmatic science of the truths of the Christian faith revealed in the Holy Scriptures. But he does not distinguish these two meanings in a sufficient manner.

---

1   Karl Barth, Church Dogmatics, I/1, trans. G.T. Thomson (Edinburgh: T & T Clark, 1936), pp. 4-5.
2   Ibid., pp. 1-47.
3   Ibid., pp. 390ff.

§ 18. Religion: the supratheoretical knowledge of God

If we wish to succeed in positing the problem concerning a Christian philosophy and its relation to dogmatic theology in a clear way, we must in the first place avoid any ambiguity in the use of the terms and define what we understand by them. We wish to establish at the outset that the true knowledge of God and of ourselves (Deum et animam scire in the Augustinian sense[1]) surpasses all theoretical thought. This knowledge cannot be the theoretical object either of a dogmatical theology or of a Christian philosophy. It can only be acquired by the operation of God's Word and the Holy Spirit in the heart – that is to say, in the religious center and root of our entire human existence and experience. True knowledge of God and self-knowledge are the central presuppositions both of a biblical theology[2] (in its scientific, theoretical sense) and, of a Christian philosophy insofar as the latter has a truly biblical starting-point. This implies that the central principle of knowledge of dogmatic theology and that of Christian philosophy ought to be the same.

From the radical and integral biblical standpoint it is [121] impossible to accept the scholastic Thomistic distinction between a natural sphere of knowledge wherein the natural light of reason is sufficient, and a supra-natural sphere, wherein our knowledge is dependent on the divine Word-revelation. This distinction testifies to a lack of real self-knowledge, caused by a departure from the biblical viewpoint. Theoretical thought is not an independent substance, as Aristotle supposed. It is always related to the I, the human self; and this ego, as the center and radical unity of our whole existence and experience, is of a religious nature [or structure]. Therefore real self-knowledge is dependent on the knowledge of God, since the ego is the central seat of the imago Dei.

Without true self-knowledge it is impossible to acquire an insight into the real relation between dogmatic theology and philosophy. For both theological and philosophical thought have their center in the same human ego. This I is the central reference point of the whole temporal order of our experience. I experience, and not some abstract sensory or intellectual function of my consciousness. Within the horizon and order of time, however, our experience displays a great diversity of fundamental aspects or experiential modes, which, as such, do not refer to a concrete what, i. e., to concrete things or events of our empirical world, but only to the how, i.e., a special manner of experiencing them.

---

1   Augustine, Soliloquies, I.ii.7.

2   I.e., a biblically-grounded dogmatic or systematic theology. As will be seen below, Dooyeweerd would think that rather than biblical theology being a 'branch' of theology as it has currently become, all theology ought to be 'biblical.'

In order to avoid the multivocality of the term "aspect" in common speech, I shall call these fundamental modes of our temporal experience, its modal [122] aspects.[1] A brief enumeration may suffice, for the present, to get a general view of the modal diversity of our experience within the order of time. Within this temporal order our experience displays a numerical aspect, a spatial aspect, an aspect of extensive movement, an aspect of energy in which we experience the physico-chemical mode of change, a biotic aspect or that of organic life, a sensitive aspect or that of feeling and sensory perception, and a logical aspect (i. e., the analytical mode of distinction in our experience lying at the foundation of our logical concepts and judgments). Further, our temporal horizon of experience displays an historical aspect, or, that of the cultural mode of development of social life, an aspect of symbolical signification lying at the foundation of all linguistic phenomena; and finally an aspect of social intercourse, an economic, an aesthetical, a juridical, a moral and a faith aspect.

All these fundamental and irreducible modalities of our experience have their common foundation in the order of time, established by the creative will of God. This order of time has arranged them in an irreversible succession and keeps them in an unbreakable mutual coherence. This is why the modal aspects of our experience are essentially modes of time, which in each of these expresses itself in a specific modal sense. Beyond the temporal horizon of our experience this diversity of modal aspects loses its sense and foundation. Neither the human I, as the religious center and radical unity of human existence, nor [123] God, whose image, according to the order of creation, finds its central expression in the human ego, are to be found within this modal diversity of our temporal horizon.

In the human ego, as the central seat of the imago Dei, God concentrated the entire meaning of the temporal world into a radical religious unity. Man, created in the image of God, should direct all the temporal functions and powers of his existence and those of his whole temporal world unto the service of God. This he was to accomplish in the central unity of his ego by loving God above all. And because, in the order of creation, every human ego in this central religious sense was united with every other human ego in a central communion of the service of God, the love for the neighbor was included in the love of God. We cannot love God without loving His image, expressed in the ego of ourselves and that of our fellow-men.[2] Therefore, the entire divine Law for God's creation displays its radical unity in the central commandment of love, addressed to the heart (i. e., religious center of human life). We

---

1   Cp. the earlier discussion above, ch. 1 (§ 2).
2   On this analysis of the 'meaning' of the self, see Augustine, De doctrina christiana, Book I.

cannot understand the radical and central sense of this commandment as long as we relate it only to the moral aspect of our temporal existence. Just as all the aspects of our temporal experience and existence find their central reference point in the human ego, so the commandment of love represents the central unity of all God's different ordinances for the temporal world. For it is not only the individual temporal existence of man which is centered in a radical unity; much [124] rather it is our whole temporal world, the "earth" as it is called in the initial words of the book of Genesis, which, according to the order of creation, finds its center in the religious root of mankind, i. e., in the spiritual community of the hearts of men in their central communion with God, the Creator.

This is the radical and integral sense of creation, according to the Word of God. It is at the same time the self-revelation of God as Creator and the revelation of man to himself as being created in God's image. It reveals to us that, even in his central position with respect to the temporal world, man is nothing in himself, but that the fullness of meaning of his existence was to be nothing short of reflecting the divine image of his Creator.

This also determines the radical and central sense of the fall into sin. This apostasy concerns the root, i.e. the religious center of human existence. The spiritual life of man depended upon his listening to the Word of God with all his heart. As soon as man closed his heart and turned away from the Word of God by giving ear to the false illusion of being something in himself (i. e., of being like God), the imago Dei was radically darkened in him and he fell prey to spiritual death. This apostasy implied the apostasy of the whole temporal world which was concentrated in man's ego. Therefore the earth was cursed, because it had no religious root of its own, but was related to the religious root or center of human existence.

For the same reason, the redemption by Jesus Christ and the communion of the Holy Spirit, which makes us into members of His body, has a central and radical sense. In Christ, mankind and the whole temporal world have received a new religious root in which the imago Dei is revealed in the fullness of its meaning.

Thus the central theme of the Holy Scriptures, namely, that of creation, fall into sin, and redemption by Jesus Christ in the communion of the Holy Spirit, has a radical unity of meaning, which is related to the central unity of our human existence. It effects the true knowledge of God and ourselves, if our heart is fully opened by the Holy Spirit so that it finds itself in the grip of God's Word and has become the captive of Jesus Christ. So long as this central meaning of the Word-revelation is at issue, we are beyond the scientific problems both of theology and philosophy. Its acceptance or rejection is a matter of life or death to us, and not a question of theoretical reflection. In this sense, the central motive of the Holy Scripture is the common supra-scientific starting-point of a truly biblical theology and of a truly Christian philosophy. It is the key of knowledge of which Jesus spoke in his discussion with the Scribes and lawyers. It is the religious presupposition of any theoretical thought, which may rightly claim a biblical foundation. But, as such, it can never become the theoretical object of theology – no more than God and the human I can become such an object.

§ 19. Theology and the critique of theoretical thought

Both theological and philosophical theoretical thought move within the boundaries of the temporal [126] order of our experience with its diversity of modal aspects. Within this temporal order the central and radical unity of the meaning of creation is, as it were, refracted into a rich diversity of modalities, just as sunlight is refracted by a prism into a rich diversity of colors. The different modal aspects of our temporal horizon of experience, which we have briefly enumerated, determine in principle the different viewpoints under which empirical reality is considered and investigated by the special sciences. This analytical dissociation of our experience in its different modal aspects, which in the pre-scientific experiential attitude is in principle lacking, is characteristic of the theoretical attitude of thought.[1] The theoretical attitude arises as soon as we begin to oppose the logical aspect of our thought to the non-logical modes of experience in order to gain a theoretical logical insight into the latter by dissociating the elements of their modal structure in an analytical way.

But these non-logical aspects offer resistance to the attempt at conceiving them in a logical manner as the theoretical objects of our logical thought. This theoretical resistance of the objects gives rise to fundamental theoretical problems of the different special sciences. The mathematical sciences, for instance, give rise to the fundamental problems: What is number? What is space? What is extensive movement? Physics and chemistry give rise to the problem: What is energy? Biology gives rise to the problem: What is organic life? Jurisprudence implies the problem: What is the [127] juridical mode of experience? And thus one could continue.

But none of these fundamental theoretical problems can be solved by these special sciences taken by themselves. They are in principle of a philosophical character. This is so because the special sciences do not reflect on their special viewpoint as such. They concentrate entirely upon the variable, actual phenomena which present themselves within the experiential aspects relating to their fields of study, at least insofar as these sciences are not of a purely mathematical character. In other words, they do not make the modal aspects of our experience them-

---

1   See ch. 1 (§ 2.b).

selves the object of their research, but only the real phenomena and then only insofar as these function in that special aspect which delimits their field of investigation. Real phenomena, however, such as concrete things, events, human acts, or communal and interpersonal relationships between men in a certain society, function in principle in all of the modal aspects of our experience. Plants and animals, for instance, present, as real perishable beings, not only a biotic aspect; they function equally in the numerical aspect, the spatial aspect, the physico-chemical aspect of energy-effect, the sensitive aspect of feeling and, sensory perception, etc. They present themselves to our pre-scientific experience in the typical structure of an individual whole. This whole functions in the unbreakable coherence of all the modal aspects of our experience; nevertheless it is typically qualified by one of these aspects. Water, for instance (in case of adequate temperature conditions), presents itself to our experience as a colorless [128] liquid matter, qualified by its physico-chemical properties. Nevertheless, it functions also in the biotic aspect or that of organic life, as a necessary means to life; it functions equally in our sensory aspect of perception, in the cultural aspect, in the economic and the juridical aspects, etc., and even in the aspect of faith. Remember, for instance, what is said in the Bible about God's dominion over the waters, which can only be experienced by faith.

When a biologist considers water, he is only concerned with its biotic aspect, i. e., its function in organic life. Nevertheless, he cannot investigate its biotical function without taking into account its physico-chemical properties. This gives rise to the fundamental theoretical problem: What is the mutual relation between the physico-chemical and the biotic aspect of the typical total-structure of a living organism? A living organism, as a real individual whole, is doubtless qualified by its biotic aspect; nevertheless, it also shows all the other aspects of our experiential world. Therefore, this fundamental problem concerning the mutual relation between the different modal aspects of an individual whole exceeds the boundaries of the special sciences and is instead one of a philosophical nature.

Let us consider another example which is of direct concern for theological science. When the theologian directs his theoretical attention to the church as an institutional organized community in our temporal world, he is confronted with a real societal whole; this whole is doubtless qualified by its faith-aspect as an institutional congregation of believers in Jesus [129] Christ. As such, the church points beyond our temporal horizon to the central religious community between Christ and the members of his body of which it should be a temporal expression. But the organized institution is not identical to this so-called invisible church. It functions as a societal whole in all the modal aspects of our temporal experiential horizon. Thus the theologian is confronted with the unbreakable coherence of the faith-aspect of this church-institution with all of its other aspects, wherein it functions as a moral, a juridical, an economic, a linguistic, a historical, a psychological, a biotic, a spatial community, etc. What is the relation between these different aspects of the church-institution, and how does this temporal communal whole relate to other communities such as the state, the family, the school, industrial organizations, trade unions, etc.?

As I said earlier, these fundamental theoretical problems exceed the boundaries of all special sciences. They are of a philosophical character, since their solution requires a theoretical total view of our temporal horizon of experience. Can Christian dogmatic theology in its own purview provide us with this philosophical total view? If so, then it cannot be a special science, but must – in line with the Augustinian conception – be considered to be identical to Christian philosophy. But this solution of the age-old problem concerning the relation between theology and philosophy is unacceptable, both from the philosophical and from the theological point of view. It is true that theology in its scientific activity comes again and again in contact [130] with other sciences, such as philology, jurisprudence, ethics, historiography, archaeology, logic, psychology, the natural sciences, etc. But this is also the case with the other special sciences. It certainly does not imply that theology therefore would be philosophy. The latter has the indispensable task of giving us an insight into the inner nature and structure of the different modal aspects of our temporal horizon of experience and to give us a theoretical view of their mutual relation and inner coherence. But theology can no more give us such a theoretical total-view than biology can. Therefore, the Thomistic distinction between philosophy and dogmatic theology constituted progress when compared with the Augustinian view which equated this theology with Christian philosophy. From the philosophical viewpoint, this equating of the two was just as unacceptable since it implies a misunderstanding of the real nature of the philosophical problems.

The criterion, however, which Thomas Aquinas used to delimit the field of philosophy from that of dogmatic theology was unserviceable in a scientific sense, and must be entirely rejected from the central biblical point of view. From the scientific viewpoint, it furnished no single insight into the true theoretical object of theology and of philosophy. Instead, it introduced the false distinction between an autonomous natural sphere of knowledge having no other source than the natural light of theoretical thought, and a supra-natural sphere dependent on divine revelation and on the supra-natural gift of faith. In this way, [131] philosophy was abandoned to the influence of central religious motives which have been unmasked by the Word of God as motives originating from the spirit of apostasy and idolatry.

As soon as we, on the basis of the central biblical standpoint, arrive with Augustine at the insight that philosophical thought cannot be self-sufficient since it is always dependent on a religious starting-point, the entire Thomistic criterion for the distinction between philosophy and theology breaks down. Nevertheless, its influence on Reformed theology has been so strong, that even Dr. Kuyper in his Encyclopedie der Heilige Godgeleerdheid,[1] was unable to extricate himself from it, although he himself had contradicted the Thomistic interpretation by calling his Encyclopedia a Christian philosophy.

It is impossible to acquire a clear insight into the relation between philosophy and theology from the biblical standpoint unless we have first arrived at a clear delimitation of the special scientific viewpoint of dogmatic theology. For it is exactly to dogmatic theology that both the Augustinian and the Thomistic tradition ascribe the exclusive right to be qualified as a Christian science. What is the proper scientific object of this theology? We shall try to find a satisfactory answer to this critical question in our second lecture [on philosophy and theology, chapter six].

---

1 Abraham Kuyper, Encyclopedie der heilige godgeleerdheid, 3 Vols. (Kampen: J.H. Kok, 1893-1894). An abridged edition is translated by J. Hendrik De Vries as Principles of Sacred Theology (Grand Rapids: Eerdmans, 1954).

Chapter Six

The Object and Task of Theology

§ 20. The object of theology as a theoretical science

a) The scientific character of theology

We concluded our first lecture [on philosophy and theology] by asking
the question: What is the proper scientific viewpoint of dogmatic theology? What is its proper theoretical object?[1] We have seen that this question cannot be answered by referring to the revelation of God in his
Word as the only true source of theological knowledge. For, as the central principle of knowledge, this Word-revelation must become the
foundation of the whole of Christian life, both in its practical and its scientific activity. In this central sense it cannot be the theoretical object of
any science, but functions only as its central starting-point, or religious
basic motive.

To find a satisfactory answer to the question at issue, we should consider that, as a science, dogmatic theology is bound to the theoretical attitude of thought. In our first lecture [chapter five] we established that
this theoretical attitude arises as soon as we begin to oppose the logical
aspect of our thought to the non-logical aspects of our experience. This
is necessary to gain a logico-theoretical insight into them, or, as in the
case of the special sciences, into a special aspect of the real facts presenting themselves within the various modes of experience. Through
this opposition of our logical [133] thought-function to the non-logical
aspect of our experience which delimits our scientific field of research,
that particular aaspect becomes the scientific object of our thought. Because of the resistance which this object offers to our attempt to gain a
systematic logico-theoretical insight into it, it gives rise to theoretical
problems. Now it has become apparent that theology cannot give us a
philosophical total view of the mutual relation and coherence between
the different aspects of our experience within the temporal order. Con-

---

1   "Object" in the sense of theology's "topic," the region or aspect which it investi-
     gates. In German one would speak of theology's Sache, its field or subject-matter.

sequently, it must be a special science.[1] In other words, the proper scientific object of dogmatic theology can only be delimited through a special modal aspect of our temporal horizon of experience. As such it must be capable of being opposed to the logical aspect of our thought as a field of theoretical problems. Nevertheless, we can only gain theoretical insight into this field by joining our logical thought-function with that special aspect of our temporal experience which delimits our scientific theological viewpoint. This modal experiential aspect that delimits the specific theological point of view can be no other than the aspect of faith.

I am well aware that this thesis may raise a complex of misunderstandings. Those who hold to the traditional way of confusing the central principle of theological knowledge with the scientific object of dogmatic theological thought will doubtless make the following objections: "By speaking of faith in the sense of a special aspect of our temporal horizon of experience [134] which delimits the particular scientific viewpoint of theology, you give evidence of a fundamental disregard for the supra-natural character of the Christian faith. This latter can never originate from human experience but is exclusively the result of the operation of the Holy Spirit in the preaching of God's Word. In addition, dogmatic theology can have no other object than the divine Word-revelation, which contains the complete doctrine of the Church. Holy Scripture cannot be understood without exegesis of its texts. This exegesis requires theological knowledge of the original texts. Consequently, Thomas Aquinas was not wrong when he said that a theological science of the divine revelation is necessary ad humanam salutem. We do not understand your distinction between the central basic motive of the Holy Scripture which would be of a supra-theological character, and the theoretical object of dogmatic theology as a science, which would be delimited by the faith-aspect of our temporal horizon of experience. How can you say that the divine revelation of creation, fall into sin, and redemption by Jesus Christ in the communion of the Holy Spirit is withdrawn from the scientific field of research in dogmatic theology? These subjects have always been the very basic materials of any theological dogmatics. Withdrawing them from the latter would amount to a complete destruction of theology."

1 A 'special science' or 'positive science' (eine positive Wissenschaft) is the science of a particular aspect of experience. Dooyeweerd's understanding of theology as a theoretical, special science converges significantly with Heidegger's development of this topic (in 1927) in Phänomenologie und Theologie (Frankfurt: Klostermann, 1970)/"Phenomenology and Theology," in The Piety of Thinking, eds. James G. Hart and John C. Maraldo (Bloomington: Indiana University Press, 1976). There Heidegger also emphasizes that "Theology is a positive science and as such is absolutely distinct from philosophy" (p. 15/7).

What shall be our answer to these serious objections: I am sorry if my explanation concerning the scientific field of research of dogmatic theology seems not clear at first sight. The difficulties and questions to which it gives rise do not concern the divine [135] Word-revelation but exclusively the scientific character and bounds of a theological dogmatics and exegesis. And it is necessary ad humanam salutem to go into these difficulties in a serious way. For dogmatic theology is a very dangerous science. Its elevation to a necessary mediator between God's Word and the believer amounts to idolatry and testifies to a fundamental misconception concerning its real character and position. If our salvation be dependent on theological dogmatics and exegesis, we are lost. For both of them are a human work, liable to all kinds of error, disagreement in opinion, and heresy.[1] We can even say that all heresies are of a theological origin. Therefore, the traditional confusion between God's Word as the central principle of knowledge and the scientific object of theological dogmatics and exegesis must be wrong in its fundamentals. For it is this very confusion which has given rise to falsely equating dogmatic theology with the doctrine of Holy Scripture, and to the false conception of theology as the necessary mediator between God's Word and the believers.

b) The transcendence of religious commitment and the limits of theology

The theoretical object of scientific thought can never be the full or integral scope of reality. The reason is that the object of theoretical thought, as such, can only result from a theoretical abstraction.[2] It originates from the theoretical dissociation of the different aspects of experience and empirical reality, which in the temporal order of the divine creation are only given in an unbreakable continuous coherence. As soon as we oppose a non-logical aspect of our experience to the theoretical logical function of our [136] thought (in order to make it into a theoretical problem), this aspect becomes the scientific object of our thought. And even if our theoretical attention is not focussed upon this aspect as such but only upon the concrete facts presenting themselves within this aspect, those concrete facts are never our theoretical object in their full reality. Rather, they are only subjected to the particular abstract scientific view-point which delimits our field of research.

---

1   For further development of the question of heresy and the status of theology within this Dooyeweerdian framework, see James K.A. Smith, "Fire From Heaven: The Hermeneutics of Heresy," Journal of TAK 20 (1996): 13-31.

2   Pretheoretical 'lived' experience exceeds the grasp of conceptual theoretical description; as such, religious commitment, as both pretheoretical and also supratheoretical, can never become an 'object' of theology as a theoretical science.

As to theology, this means that the divine Word-revelation can never become the theoretical object of theological research in the full reality wherein it presents itself to us. In its central religious sense it addresses itself to the heart, to the religious center of our existence, as a divine spiritual power, and not as an object of theological reflection. Therefore, the basic theme of Holy Scripture, namely that of creation, fall into sin and redemption by Jesus Christ in the communion of the Holy Spirit, can never become the scientific object of theology in this central religious sense. As such it is much rather the supra-theological starting-point of all truly biblical Christian thought, the key to the knowledge of God and of ourselves.[1] But within the temporal order of our experience this Word-revelation manifests itself in the same modal diversity of aspects we find in our own temporal human existence. God's Word has entered our temporal horizon, just as it has become flesh in Jesus Christ, our Savior. And it is only within the temporal diversity of experiential aspects that the divine revelation can become an object of theological thought. [137]

It cannot be doubted that the temporal order of our experience, according to the divine order of creation, has a limiting aspect of faith, which in this sense is a fundamental mode of experience, clearly distinct from all other modes. The modal structure of this aspect, which determines its irreducible meaning, belongs to the order of creation, and could, as such, not be affected by sin. Sin cannot destroy anything of God's creation, it can only give to it a false, apostate direction.[2] Both genuine Christian faith and apostate faith, and even unbelief, can only function within the same modal aspect of faith which is inherent in the created temporal order of our experience. They all have a fundamental faith character, just as both the legal and illegal manner of behavior are of a juridical character and both a logical and an illogical manner of reasoning can only occur within the logical aspect of thought. But the modal faith-aspect may not be equated with the real act of believing which in its full reality comes out of the heart and, though qualified by its faith-aspect, also presents other aspects in the temporal order of experience. It is beyond discussion that the actual Christian faith in its true sense can only originate from the operation of God's Word, as a central

---

1   The "Word-revelation" transcends the temporal order of experience and thus cannot be objectified by theoretical thought which operates within the temporal horizon. However, the divine Word-revelation does "manifest" itself within that order (e.g., in the Scriptures); it is these temporal, concrete manifestations which are investigated by theology.

2   Faith, for Dooyeweerd, is creational; that is, it is part of being a creature rather than a postlapsarian 'remedy.' As such, it is part of the structure of creation which, after the Fall, can take an apostate direction. See also the discussion of idolatry ch. 2, § 6.

spiritual power, in the heart, i. e., the religious center of our existence.[1] But this does not detract from the fact that it functions within the modal faith-aspect of our temporal experience which belongs to the temporal order of creation.

c)   God's revelations and the possibility of theology

Now it should be considered that this faith-aspect occupies [138] an entirely exceptional place in the order of creation; it is the limiting aspect that even in the kernel of its modal sense refers beyond the temporal order to the religious center of our existence and to the divine Origin of all that has been created. This modal kernel of the faith-aspect may be circumscribed as that ultimate mode of certitude within the temporal order of experience which refers to an indubitable revelation of God touching us in the religious center of our existence.[2] Now, the living God has revealed himself in the whole of his creation, in all the works of his hands.[3] But this revelation, which in the temporal order displays a rich diversity of aspects, finds its center of operation in the heart, the center and root of human existence, wherein God has expressed the central meaning of his image. And it is the faith-aspect in its modal meaning through which the divine revelation within the temporal order of our experience is related to this religious center of our consciousness and existence.

We should, however, consider that from the very beginning this revelation of God in all the works of his hands was not open to a would-be autonomous human understanding. This phanerosis, as it is called in the first chapter of the Epistle to the Romans (1:19), was elucidated and interpreted by the Word of God that addressed itself to the heart of man by mediation of the temporal function of faith. So long as the human heart was open to the Word of God, man was capable of understanding the sense of God's general[4] phanerosis by means of his innate function of faith. But as soon as this heart closed itself and turned away from

---

1   With existentialists such as Pascal and Kierkegaard, Dooyeweerd shares an understanding of the human self as more than rational; thus, 'conversion' is not understood as intellectual assent to theological propositions, but rather the existential commitment of the 'heart' as the "religious center of our existence." The self is not, for Dooyeweerd, homo rationale but rather homo religionis. See also ch. 2 and ch. 7.

2   In subsequent scholarship, the 'pistic' or 'faith aspect' has also been described as the certitudinal aspect. However, this is not a Cartesian certainty, but rather what Herman Bavinck described as the certainty of faith – a contradiction in terms from a Cartesian standpoint. See Herman Bavinck, The Certainty of Faith, trans. Harry der Nederlanden (St. Catharines: Paideia Press, 1980).

3   For Calvin's discussion of 'general revelation' in creation, see Institutes, I.v. For a commentary, see Susan E. Schreiner, The Theater of His Glory: Nature and the Natural Order in the Thought of John Calvin (Durham: Labyrinth Press, 1991).

4   Both Catholic and Reformed theology have made a traditional distinction between God's "general" or "natural" revelation in the works of creation, and his "special" revelation in the Scriptures. For a history of the concept of general revelation, see

[139] the Word of God as a result of its apostasy, the faith-aspect of the temporal human experience was also closed. It was no longer the window of our temporal experience, open to the light of eternity, but it became the instrument of the spirit of apostasy.[1] Likewise the innate religious impulsion of the human heart to transcend itself in order to find rest in its divine origin began to unfold itself in an idolatrous direction. It is exclusively by the operation of the Holy Spirit which regenerates the heart that the faith-aspect of our temporal experience can be re-opened to the Word of God, so that its negative direction is changed into a positive one. Thus it is completely true that the living Christian faith can in no way originate from the temporal experience of man who because of his apostasy has fallen prey to spiritual death.[2]

§ 21. Faith and the relationship between nature and grace

a) Scholastic dualism

Nevertheless, its modal structure and general faith-character belong to the temporal order of human experience as it is founded in the divine creation. Consequently, even Christian faith does not result from a completely new creative act of God, as Barth thinks.[3] Therefore the scholastic Roman Catholic view of faith as a supra-natural gift of God to the human intellect,[4] manifesting itself beyond the natural order of creation, should also be rejected from the biblical standpoint. It is only under the influence of the dualistic religious motive of nature and grace that scholastic theology introduced this conception. But this motive which has continued to rule both Roman Catholic theology and Protestant scholasticism, is of [140] an unbiblical origin. It is a dialectical basic motive aiming at an accommodation of the central motive of Holy Scripture to religious motives of an apostate character, either to that of Greek philosophy or to that of modern Humanism. This dualistic basic motive has deprived scholastic theology of the insight into the radical and integral

---

Bruce A. Demarest, General Revelation: Historical Views and Contemporary Issues (Grand Rapids: Zondervan, 1982).

1   In contrast to the Catholic tradition following Thomas, the Reformational tradition has emphasized that the general revelation of God in creation is no longer acknowledged because of the noetic effects of sin. While the Catholic tradition points to Romans 1:20, the Reformational tradition reads this in light of Romans 1:19, which indicates that this truth is suppressed and is no longer acknowledged by people. There is, properly speaking, no Reformational 'natural' theology. For Calvin's seminal discussion, see Institutes, I.i-vi.

2   Here and below, Dooyeweerd is answering the objection posed earlier, that his understanding of the faith aspect 'naturalizes' faith and regeneration.

3   Barth, Church Dogmatics, I/1, pp. 260-283.

4   See, for example, Thomas Aquinas, Summa Theologiae, IaIIae.85.1-2, IIaIIae.5.1 (on loss of grace and faith as the effect of sin) and IIaIIae.6.1-2 (on the supernatural 'infusion' of faith).

character of the Word-revelation. It has led to a theological conception of human nature which has no room for the heart as the religious center and radical unity of human existence.[1] By ascribing to the so-called natural reason an autonomy over against faith and divine revelation, traditional scholastic theology merely gave expression to the false Greek view of reason as the center of human nature. Within the framework of the Roman Catholic ecclesiastic doctrine this caused no inner difficulties, since this doctrine did not accept the radical character of the fall into sin.[2]

In Reformed theology, on the other hand, this unbiblical view of human nature could not fail to cause an inner contradiction with the biblical doctrine of sin and redemption. For, if human nature does not have a religious center or radix, how can the fall be of a radical character, i. e., touch the root of our nature? Sin cannot originate from man's intellect. If the latter would be the center of our human nature, independent from our central religious life, it would not be affected by sin. Therefore, Roman Catholic doctrine was consistent when it denied the inner corruption of human nature. And it is this very view of human nature which caused the problem of the relation [141] between theology and philosophy to be posed on a fundamentally erroneous basis. The whole distinction between a so-called sacred theology and the so-called secular sciences issued from the unbiblical dualism inherent in the scholastic basic motive of nature and supra-natural grace.

b) Barth's dualism

It is a heartening symptom of a re-awakening biblical consciousness that, under the influence of Augustinianism, an increasing number of Roman Catholic thinkers, belonging to the movement of the so-called nouvelle théologie,[3] have begun to oppose this dualistic view. They agree with the Reformed philosophical movement in the Netherlands in advocating the necessity of a Christian philosophy. On the other hand, we must observe that the Barthian view of theology as the exclusive Christian science and with its negative relation to philosophy, is still entirely penetrated by this dualism. This is a baffling situation since, in

---

1 Dooyeweerd, like Pascal, always points to the 'heart' as the center of human existence, precisely to delimit the rationalism which has dominated Western theology, particularly in the scholasticism (both Catholic and Protestant) with which he is concerned here. Rationalism, on Dooyeweerd's terms, is both an absolutization of one aspect from the temporal order, as well as a reduction of the multi-dimensionality of the human self.

2 That is, faith was understood to be a supernatural supplement lost at the Fall. 'Nature' thus remains unaffected by sin. As mentioned earlier, see Thomas Aquinas, Summa Theologiae, IaIIae.85.1-2, IIaIIae.5.1 (on loss of grace and faith as the effect of sin) and IIaIIae.6.1-2 (on the supernatural 'infusion' of faith).

3 A movement in Catholic theology in France in the 1960s which both influenced and was influenced by Vatican II.

sharp contrast to Roman Catholicism, Barth claims for his theology a radical biblical character. How is this to be explained? The reason is that Barth, though sharply opposed to the synthetical Thomistic view of nature and grace, did not abandon this dualistic theme itself; a scheme which in the Augustinian view was still unknown. He merely replaced its synthetical conception, according to which nature is the autonomous basis of the supra-natural sphere of grace, by an antithetical one which denies any point of contact between the corrupted autonomous nature and the divine work of grace. Thus philosophy was excommunicated as such, because by nature it would be [142] an autonomous product of natural thought which is corrupted by sin. Among all the sciences only dogmatic theology was supposed to be capable of being permeated by the Word-revelation. In my opinion, this dualistic view betrays the after-effects of the Occamistic Nominalism, which has especially influenced the Lutheran view concerning the impossibility of a Christian philosophy.

However, if the possibility of a Christian philosophy is denied, one should also deny the possibility of a Christian theology in the sense of a science of the biblical doctrine. Barth, however, emphatically maintains this scientific character of theology, though, in complete accordance with Thomas Aquinas, he places all stress on its supra-natural principle of knowledge. But he admits that this theology is obliged to avail itself of the same theoretical thought as philosophy does. How, then, can this theological thought claim a Christian character? Luther called natural reason a harlot which is blind, deaf, and dumb with respect to the truths revealed in the Word of God. But, if this prostitute can become a saint by its subjection to the Word of God, it is hard to understand why this miracle would only occur within the sphere of theological dogmatics. Why may not philosophical thought also be ruled by the central motive of Holy Scripture? It is certainly not the biblical basic motive in its radical and integral sense which led many theologians to the conclusion that philosophy has nothing to do with the Kingdom of God. It is only the non-biblical dualistic motive of nature and grace that led them astray and that inspired Barth's view that man may expect that, at least in general, God has bound the operation of his Word to a "theological space" in which the Bible, ecclesiastical preaching, and theology, as to their instrumental function, are placed on the same level. It is this scholastic basic-motive which has also impeded the necessary transcendental critique of theological thought, both as to its scientific object and as to its starting point.

§ 22. The relation between the Scriptures and the Word-revelation

We have already noted that the appropriate object of dogmatic theological thought can only be found within the temporal order of experience. We have established that that object cannot be anything but the Divine Word-revelation as that revelation presents itself within the modal aspect of faith. This latter is made into a theological problem in the theoretical attitude of thought by being placed over against the logical function of theological thinking. We must now try to realize the significance of the distinction between the Word of God in its full and actual reality and in its restricted sense as the object of theological thought. This is necessary in order to answer the question as to whether it is true that this distinction would withdraw from theological dogmatics its chief subject-matter, which would amount to a complete destruction of dogmatic theology in its traditional sense.[1]

a) The Scriptures as a temporal manifestation of the Word-revelation

Let us first consider how the Word of God presents itself to us in its full and actual reality. The divine Word-revelation has entered our temporal horizon. The Word was made flesh and dwelt among us (John 1:14). This was the skandalon (1 Cor. 1:23) which was equally raised by the [144] incarnation of the Word-revelation in the Holy Scriptures, a collection of books written by different men in the course of ages; divinely inspired, yet related to all the modal aspects of our temporal horizon of experience. It is, however, only under the modal aspect of faith that we can experience that this Word-revelation in the Scriptures has indeed been inspired by the Holy Spirit. And the actual belief through which we know with an ultimate certainty that it is so, cannot be realized in the heart, that religious center of our consciousness, except by the operation of the Word itself, as a spiritual power.[2] What then makes the diversity of books of the Old and New Testament into a radical spiritual unity? Their principle of unity can only be found in the central theme of creation, fall into sin, and redemption by Jesus Christ in the communion of the Holy Spirit, since it is the key to true knowledge of God and self-knowledge.

We have established that, in its central spiritual sense, as divine motive power addressing itself to our heart, this theme cannot become the theoretical object of theological thought, since it is the very starting

---

1   This was one of the theologians' predictable objections Dooyeweerd referred to earlier in his remarks: if the Word-revelation cannot be an object for theological consideration, then does that not eliminate theology altogether?

2   Calvin emphasizes this same point: Scripture's authority is 'self-authenticating' (autopistic), confirmed by the witness of the Spirit in the heart, not rational arguments posed to the intellect. See Institutes I.vii.

point for such thought, at least if theology is to be truly biblical. But dogmatic theology can doubtless engage in a theoretical reflection on creation, fall into sin, and redemption, insofar as their revelation is related to the faith aspect of our temporal experience and forms the contents of articles of Christian belief. It is even possible for a theologian to do so from a non-biblical starting point, such as the traditional scholastic [145] basic-motive of nature and grace. Starting from this unbiblical motive, Thomas Aquinas considered creation as a partly natural philosophical and partly supra-natural truth. The fall was taken as merely the loss of the supra-natural gift of grace, which did not corrupt the rational nature of man, but only wounded it. This theological view of creation and fall was sanctioned as orthodox doctrine by the Roman Catholic Church.

b) Religious commitment and the articles of faith

From the foregoing it may appear that there must be a difference in principle between creation, fall and redemption in their central sense as the key to knowledge, and in their sense as articles of faith which may be made into the object of theological thought. Insofar as Reformed theology, too, was influenced by the scholastic basic motive of nature and grace, it also developed dogmatic views which must be considered unbiblical. The Jewish Scribes and lawyers had a perfect theological knowledge of the books of the Old Testament. They wished, doubtless, to hold to the creation, the fall and the promise of the coming Messiah as articles of the orthodox Jewish faith which are also articles of the Christian faith. Nevertheless, Jesus said to them: "Woe unto you, for ye have taken away the key of knowledge!" (Luke 11:52). This key of knowledge in its radical and integral sense cannot be made into a theological problem. The theologian can only direct his theological thought to it with respect to its necessary supra-theoretical presupposition, if he is really in the grip of it and can bear witness to its radical meaning which transcends all theological [146] concepts. But when he does so, he is in not in any different position than the Christian philosopher who accounts for his biblical starting-point, or the ordinary believer who testifies to the radical sense of God's Word as the central motive power of his life in Jesus Christ. In other words, the true knowledge of God in Jesus Christ and true self-knowledge are neither of a dogmatic-theological, nor of a philosophical nature, but have an absolutely central religious significance. This knowledge is a question of spiritual life or death. Even orthodox theological dogmatics, however splendidly elaborated, cannot guarantee this central spiritual knowledge. Therefore, the scholastic term sacra theologia testifies to an unbiblical over-estimation of theology.[1] All theological problems such as the significance of the

---

1   Dooyeweerd transcendental critique of theology is a critique in the Kantian sense of a delimitation, an analysis which marks the limits and boundaries of science (knowl-

imago Dei before and after the fall, the relation between creation and sin and that of particular grace to common grace, that of the union of the two natures in Jesus Christ, etc., can only arise in the theoretical opposition of the faith-aspect to the logical aspect of our thought. They are certainly legitimate problems of theological dogmatics, but as specifically theological problems they do not concern the central basic motive of the Holy Scriptures as it is operative in the religious center of our consciousness and existence. This spiritual basic motive is elevated above all theological controversies and is not in need of theological exegesis, since its radical meaning is exclusively explained by the Holy Spirit operating in our opened hearts, in the communion of this Spirit. This is the only really ecumenical basis of the Church of Christ, which in its institutional temporal appearance is otherwise hopelessly divided. And it is the ultimate divine judge both of all dogmatic theology and of all philosophy. This does not mean that this spiritual basic motive would be the basis of a Christendom above all dissensions of faith as though it would not have any connection with an ecclesiastical confession. On the contrary, it is also the judge of every ecclesiastical doctrine and will always remain the central basic principle of a continual reformation of the Church's doctrine. Every view which makes this central and radical sense of God's Word dependent on a theological dogmatics and exegesis is unbiblical in its very fundamentals.

§ 23. The relation and distinction between theology and Christian philosophy

a)   Their shared basic-motive and distinct fields

This radical biblical standpoint lies at the foundation of the reformed philosophy which during the past four decades has been developed at the Free University of Amsterdam. It has inspired its radical critique of theoretical thought which applies both to philosophy itself and to theology. This critique, which is the key to an understanding of its philosophical intent and significance, has uncovered the inner point of connection between theoretical thought, in all of its manifestations, and the central religious basic motives which are its real, but often masked, starting-points. It has done so by showing from the inner structure and nature of theoretical thought itself its necessary presuppositions which are necessarily related to the central religious sphere of human consciousness. This means that the traditional dogma concerning the auton-

edge). Thus, Dooyeweerd relativizes the status of theology: as a theoretical science, it must remain distinct from faith, which is pretheoretical. We might keep the two distinct by reserving the term religion for the pre- and supra-theoretical commitments of faith, and employing the term theology only in the technical sense as a theoretical investigation of the faith aspect and Word-revelation as it is manifested in the temporal horizon. As above, this relativization of the status of theology emphasizes that 'salvation' is not a matter of theology but rather of religion, understood as existential commitment.

omy of theoretical reason with respect to the natural truths turns out to be untenable. It is the central religious motive of theoretical [148] thought which, as its real starting-point, rules any philosophical view of the mutual relation and inner coherence between the different aspects of our temporal horizon of experience. This is why the biblical basic-motive cannot fail to bring about a salutary inner revolution in our entire philosophical view of temporal experience and of empirical reality. Neither philosophy, nor dogmatic theology, can be withdrawn from the radical and integral grip of this central basic-motive without being abandoned to the influence of non-biblical motives.

b) The philosophical foundations of theology

However, Christian philosophy does not have the task and competence to go into the dogmatic an exegetical problems of theology except insofar as the philosophical and central religious fundamentals of theology as a theoretical science are at issue. For as soon as the fatal confusion between the central starting-point and the theoretical object of theology has been overcome, it must be evident that theology in its scientific sense is bound to philosophical fundamentals[1] which are in turn dependent on the central religious motive of theoretical thought. The reason is that the faith-aspect of our temporal horizon of experience, which delimits the theoretical object of theology in its modal sense, displays an intrinsic coherence with all the other experiential modes. This inner coherence between the different aspects finds expression in the modal structure of each of them, so that this structure reflects the integral temporal order of all the aspects in their established succession. This implies that the modal structure of the faith-aspect, [149] just like that of all other experiential modes, displays an intricate character. On the one hand, it presents a central moment of its sense [meaning], which is its irreducible kernel. On the other, it displays a series of analogical moments, whose meaning is in itself multivocal and is only determined by the modal kernel of the faith-aspect. The analogical moments give expression to the inner coherence between this aspect and all the other modes of experience within the temporal order.[2]

It is this analogical structure of the faith-aspect which obliges theology to avail itself of fundamental concepts of an analogical character. That is to say, these concepts are also used by the other special sciences, but in a different modal sense; nevertheless, there is an inner coherence between these different modal meanings. Such theological concepts of

---

1   Heidegger, in a manner almost identical to Dooyeweerd, emphasizes that theology as a positive science must operate from a philosophical foundation which provides it with is "basic concepts" (Grundbegriffen). See Phänomenologie und Theology, pp. 27-33/17-21. So also below, Dooyeweerd asserts that theology must "avail itself of fundamental concepts of an analogical character."

2   For a discussion of "analogical moments," see ch. 4, § 14.

an analogical character are, for instance, those of time, number, space, movement, force and causality, life, emotion, distinction, power, symbol, signification and interpretation, justice, guilt, imputation and punishment, love, etc. It is of primordial concern that the theologian realizes the proper faith-sense of these analogical concepts in their theological use and does not confound this particular signification with that ascribed to them in other sciences. For such confusion cannot fail to give rise to erroneous ways of posing theological problems.

I refer, for example, to the question concerning the sense of the six days of creation. By disregarding the faith-aspect of the temporal order and by utilizing astronomical and geological concepts of time, theology was entangled [150] in the following [pseudo-theological] dilemma: if these days are not to be understood in the sense of astronomical days of twenty-four hours, then they ought to be interpreted as geological periods. A curious dilemma, indeed.[1] For it has not occurred to any theologian to apply this alternative to the seventh day, the day on which God rests from all his work which he had wrought. Such an interpretation would be rightly considered blasphemous. But why was it overlooked that the same blasphemy presents itself if God's creative deeds are conceived of in natural scientific time-concepts? The reason is that the theologians who posed the aforementioned dilemma did not realize the fundamental difference between the divine creative deeds and the genetic process occurring within the created temporal order as a result of God's work of creation. Here the influence of Greek philosophy clearly manifested itself. For because of its pagan religious basic motive, this philosophy excluded any idea of creation. It merely accepted a temporal genesis, at most conceived of as the result of a formative activity of a divine mind which presupposes a given material. The scholastic accommodation of the biblical revelation of creation to this Greek idea of becoming gave rise to the false view that creation itself was a temporal process.

God's creative deeds surpass the temporal order because they are not subjected to it. But as a truth of faith God has revealed these creative deeds in the faith-aspect of this temporal order which points beyond itself to what is supra-temporal. It was God's will that the believing Jew should refer his six work [151] days to the six divine creative works and the sabbath day to the eternal sabbatic rest of God, the Creator. This is the biblical exegesis given by the Decalogue. And it eliminates the scholastic dilemma concerning the exegesis of the six days of creation, which originated from a fundamental disregard of the faith-aspect of the temporal order. This disregard is also to be observed in the Augustinian

1   Dooyeweerd would view any form of scientific creationism as an interpretation of Genesis 1-2 which fails to understand the meaning of 'day' within the faith-aspect, thereby reducing it to the physical aspect.

103

interpretation of the six days as a literary form or framework of representation which lacks any temporal sense, though this conception is, no doubt, preferable by far to the astronomical or geological interpretation.

Theological pseudo-problems always arise when the analogical basic theological concepts are used in a non-theological sense. Remember, for instance, the Occamistic conception of God's omnipotence as an absolute power separate from God's justice, love, holiness, etc. In this way the analogical concept of power was conceived in the sense of a tyrannical arbitrariness, and certainly not in the sense of the Christian faith. Power in its original modal sense is the nuclear moment of the historico-cultural mode of experience; for culture is nothing but a controlling mode of formation, which specifically by virtue of its qualification as having dominion over material things is fundamentally distinct from all modes of formation found in nature.

But even in this original and nuclear modal sense power is only to be conceived of in unbreakable coherence with the whole series of analogical experiential moments in the historico-cultural aspect in which the context with the other aspects finds expression. Similarly, the analogy [152] of power which we encounter in the modal structure of the faith-aspect cannot unfold its analogical meaning within this aspect apart from its unbreakable coherence with all the other analogies in this mode of experience. Any attempt to isolate such an analogy and to relate it in this isolation to God as a predicate of his self-revelation, amounts to an absolutization of a temporal moment of our experience. It leads to the formation of idols which results in a meaningless nothingness. In the same way the theological meaning of the analogical concept of causality is misunderstood by conceiving predestination in a mechanical sense. Nevertheless, the theological meaning of all these [analogical] concepts can only reveal itself in the unbreakable coherence of the faith-aspect with all the other aspects of the temporal order of experience.

c)   *A radically Christian philosophy as the only*
     foundation for a Christian theology

This is the reason why theology in its scientific sense needs a philosophical foundation. For it is philosophy alone which can provide us with a theoretic insight into the inner structure and the mutual coherence of the different aspects or modes of human experience. The only question is whether these philosophical fundamentals will be subject to the biblical religious basic motive or to some non-biblical religious basic motive originating from a complete or partial apostasy. It is only the radical and integral biblical starting-point which can free philosophy from prejudices that imply a distortion of the structural order of the experiential aspects. The apostate basic-motives cannot fail to entangle philosophic thought in the absolutization of specific aspects, whereby an [153] insight into their real structure and real coherence with the others is precluded in principle. It is a vain illusion to imagine that such philosophical views could be made harmless by accommodating them in an external way to the ecclesiastical doctrine to which the theologian holds.

By a lasting tradition, originating in the canonization of the Thomistic view, but already prepared by pre-Thomistic scholasticism, dogmatic theology has been bound to a scholastic philosophy ruled by the unbiblical basic motive of nature and grace. In fact, it was an Aristotelian philosophy accommodated to the doctrine of the Church. The analogical character of the theological basic concepts was conceived from the viewpoint of the Aristotelian metaphysics, which started from the analogical concept of being, the so-called analogia entis. But this metaphysics, howsoever accommodated to the Church's doctrine, could not fail to turn away theological thought from the radical biblical standpoint since its basic motive was incompatible with that of the Holy Scripture. I shall revert to this point in my next lecture [chapter seven]. By means of the metaphysical doctrine of the analogia entis dogmatic theology tried to account for the fact that Holy Scripture speaks about God in terms related to the modal diversity of our temporal order of experience. But this doctrine of the analogia entis had nothing to do with the Christian faith. Rather, it was supposed to be founded on natural reason alone in its pretended autonomy.

Karl Barth rightly rejected this metaphysics of the analogia entis. He called it an invention of the antichrist and replaced it by the analogia fidei, the analogy of faith.[1] But, as we have seen, it is exactly the analogical structure of faith which confronts theology with a basic problem of a philosophical character that cannot be put aside. If, as Barth thinks, Christian belief would really have no single point of contact with human nature, how can it display that analogical structure by which it is bound even to the sensory aspect of our experience? How could we believe without having first heard the Word with the ear of sense, or without having first perceived the written words of the Bible with the eye of sense and having understood the lingual meaning of the words? It is this very coherence of the faith aspect with all the other fundamental modes of temporal experience which cannot be explained from the theological view-point alone.

If the theologians deny the possibility of a biblically-founded philosophy, they are bound to take their philosophical presuppositions from a so-called autonomous philosophy. It is a vain illusion to imagine that the notions borrowed from such a philosophy could be utilized by the theologian in a purely formal sense. They involve a material content which is indissolubly bound to the total theoretical view of experience

---

1 Barth, Church Dogmatics, I/1, pp. 279-281.

and of reality. It has been pretended, for instance, that the philosophical concept of substance could be utilized by theology in a formal sense to give expression to the essential unity of soul and body in human nature.[1] Yet, this metaphysical concept contained a Greek view of human nature which excluded in principle the insight into the religious center of human existence. How could theology, on such a philosophical basis, do justice to the revelation of creation in its radical biblical sense? How could it do justice to the pregnant biblical pronouncements concerning the heart as the inner center of human life?

And the situation does not improve if theology turns away from the scholastic-Aristotelian philosophy in order to have recourse to modern philosophical views rooted in the basic motive of Humanism. In Europe there are many theologians who consider the contemporary humanist existentialism more biblical than Aristotelianism. I do not understand this opinion. The qualification "more biblical" is characteristic of the neo-scholastic attitude in theological and philosophical thought which only aims at an accommodation of this uprooted humanist existentialism to the biblical view without having realized the radical and integral character of the biblical basic motive. Genuine Humanistic basic views concerning man and his world that have a more or less biblical character do not exist. The biblical basic motive can only be accepted or rejected as a whole. And the same applies to the Humanist religious position. Naturally this does not mean that important elements of truth are not to be found in humanist existentialism. But the philosophical total view from which such elements are interpreted does not leave room for partial acceptance of this philosophy from the biblical standpoint. It is an integral [156] whole, ruled by the religious basic motive of Humanism.

Theology is above all in need of a radical critique of theoretical thought which, because of its biblical starting-point, is able to show the intrinsic influence of the religious basic motives both upon philosophy and theology. This is the first service which the new reformed philosophy can render its theological sister. In my next lecture [chapter seven] I shall explain the necessity of this service in more detail.

---

1   See, for example, Aquinas, ST, Ia.75-76.

Chapter Seven

Reformation and Scholasticism in Theology

§ 24. The grounding of scholasticism in non-biblical basic motives

a) Dialectical tensions

In the last lecture [chapter six] I showed why theology as a science of the dogmata of the Christian faith is in need of a philosophical foundation. Without a doubt, the Christian life of faith as such does not need philosophy, nor does the divine Word-revelation.[1] Neither of them is of a theoretical character. Dogmatical theology, on the contrary, is in its scientific character bound to the theoretical attitude of thought. It is continually confronted with the problem concerning the relation between its analogical basic concepts to those of the other sciences. As we have seen, this problem appears to have an inner connection with the place which the faith aspect of our experience occupies in the temporal order of the experiential aspects. And this problem is of an intrinsically philosophical nature.

For theology, the question is not whether or not it should be philosophically founded; the only question is whether it is to seek its philosophical foundations in a Christian philosophy, ruled and reformed by the central biblical basic-motive or whether it should take them from the traditional scholastic or modern Humanist philosophy. [158] The influence of the scholastically-adapted Greek philosophy on dogmatic theology was, as I stated, the more dangerous since the theologians – led

---

1 It is theology as a theoretical science that requires a philosophical foundation; faith, as a pretheoretical commitment, does not stand in need of a theoretical foundation. Heidegger emphasizes that "faith does not need philosophy" (Phänomenologie und Theologie, p. 27/17). Heidegger, however, unlike Dooyeweerd, also understands faith and philosophy as "mortal enemies" (pp. 32/20). For a critique of Heidegger from a Dooyeweerdian perspective, see James K.A. Smith, "The Art of Christian Atheism: Faith and Philosophy in Early Heidegger," Faith and Philosophy 14 (1997): 71-81.

astray by the traditional belief in the autonomy of natural reason – did not realize the anti-biblical presuppositions of this philosophy.

We should not forget that the process of decay of Reformation theology had begun with the restoration of this scholastic philosophy at the Protestant universities. This restoration effectuated by Melanchton and Beza, meant (unintentionally of course) a denial of the integral principle of the Reformation with its implicaiton of an inner reformation of the whole of Christian life by its subjection to the radical and central authority of God's Word-revelation. It testified to the fact that the un-biblical religious basic motive of nature and grace had begun to regain a growing influence on the theological and philosophical views of Protestantism. The Roman Catholic view in its Thomistic conception – according to which philosophy can have no other principle of knowledge than the natural light of reason, whereas theology has a supra-natural source of knowledge in revelation – was completely taken over. But the return to this view implied a return to the scholastic foundation of dogmatic theology on the metaphysical fundamentals of the Aristotelian philosophy in its external accommodation to the doctrine of the Church. This meant that any attack upon the Aristotelian metaphysics was rightly felt as an attack upon the scholastic trend in Reformed theology itself. And insofar as the influence of [159] the Thomistic-Aristotelian metaphysics had even revealed itself in some formulations of the Reformed Confessions, especially in the Westminster Confession, this attack could be easily interpreted as a deviation from the Church's doctrine. But in doing so an inescapable difficulty arose.

The Thomistic-Aristotelian view of human nature, which excluded the biblical revelation of the heart as the religious center of human life, was supposed to give expression both to a philosophical and to a theological truth. As a philosophical conception it was supposed to be provable by the natural light of reason alone; as a theological conception it sought support from different texts of Holy Scripture, which were supposed to corroborate it. This implied that a philosophical anthropology was ascribed to the Holy Scriptures – an anthropology, which was incompatible with the radical sense of the biblical revelation concerning creation, fall and redemption. But by making such an ascription the only criterion at the disposal of Scholasticism for delimiting the field of research of theology from that of philosophy, appeared to be negated. The only means to escape from effacing the bounds between them was to forbid the philosophers any independent consultation of the Holy Scriptures and to bind them to the Thomistic-Aristotelian view of human nature.

b) Attempted solutions

This solution of the difficulty was quite Roman Catholic, and it presupposed the Roman Catholic view of the infallible doctrinal authority of
the Church. The Reformation, however, had rejected this authority in
principle and had opened the Bible to [160] all believers. In consequence, until the separation of church and state, there seemed to remain
no other escape than that the church apply for help to the secular government in case of disagreement between philosophers and theologians
about anthropological questions.

This road was followed in the Netherlands in the 17th century, when
the contest between the adherents of the Cartesian philosophy and the
theologians at the universities had led to serious troubles. The Carte-
sians defended the thesis that the material body and the rational soul are
only accidentally united in human nature. The theologians held to the
Thomistic-Aristotelian view of a substantial union between these two
components. In the year 1656 the Estate of Holland and West-Friesland
issued their famous resolution concerning the relation between philosophy and theology in consequence of a complain lodged by the Synod of
the Dutch Reformed Churches against the propagation of the Cartesian
views with respect to subjects belonging to theology. This resolution
began by applying the traditional scholastic criterion in order to delimit
the bounds of philosophy and theology. Philosophy should restrict itself
to questions which may be investigated by the natural light of reason
alone; theology, on the other hand should treat such subjects which are
to be known only from the Word-revelation.

It was evident that a consistent application of this criterion could not
fail to lead to the conclusion that the theological professors should abstain from teaching [161] any philosophical theory of man. But this
would have been unacceptable from the theological viewpoint, since the
Thomistic-Aristotelian view of human nature was considered to be in
accordance with the doctrine of Holy Scripture and thus was made into
an article of faith. On the other hand, the question at issue could not be
withdrawn from philosophy and assigned to the exclusive competence
of theology. For both the scholastic philosophy, defended by the theologians, and the Cartesian philosophy, considered it as belonging to the
essential problems of metaphysics. Consequently, the resolution of the
Estates was obliged to take these difficulties into account. It established
that theology has borrowed many terms, distinctions, and rules from
other sciences, which in many respects can help to clarify the theological problems. On the other hand, it admitted that there are subjects
which, though belonging also to the realm of faith, nevertheless may be
examined and known by the natural light of reason alone. Therefore, the
resolution recommended to the philosophers that they treat such sub-

jects less amply than the theologians who used arguments taken from the Holy Scriptures, the exegesis of texts, the refutation of older and contemporary heresies, etc. Besides, according to the resolution, such matters can be understood much better and more securely from the Holy Scriptures than from natural reason. Consequently, when the natural light of human reason would seem to lead us to other results, one should have more confidence in the divine authority alone [162] than in human reasoning. On these grounds the resolution prohibited a further propagation of the Cartesian theses which had given offense to the theologians. In this way the secular government tried to put an end to the debate between the Cartesian philosophers and the theologians. But the resolution – which satisfied the wishes of the ecclesiastics – and followed, in the main, the advice of the theological faculty of the University of Leyden, showed at the same time to what degree the spirit of Scholasticism had supplanted the biblical spirit of the Reformation. The Thomist view of human nature as a composite of an immortal, rational soul and a perishable material body united as form and matter of one substance, had no more in common with the biblical revelation about man than the Cartesian conception. Both of them were metaphysical theories ruled by un-biblical religious basic motives.

The whole idea that a philosophical knowledge of human nature would be possible by the natural light of human reason alone (i. e., independent of religious presuppositions) testified to a fundamental apostasy from the biblical starting-point. And the very fact that scholastic theology sought to corroborate the Thomistic-Aristotelian view by texts of the Scripture showed to what a great extent theological exegesis itself had come into the grip of un-biblical basic motives.

§ 25. The Greek foundations of scholasticism

a) The matter-motive in Greek religion

Let us consider this situation in a little more detail. The nature-grace motive did not enter Christian thought before the end of the 12th century, during the renaissance of the Aristotelian philosophy. It aimed originally at a religious compromise between the Aristotelian view of nature and the ecclesiastical doctrine of creation, fall into sin, and redemption by Jesus Christ. But the Aristotelian view of nature was no more independent of religious presuppositions than any other philosophical view. It was completely ruled by the dualistic religious basic motive of Greek thought, namely, that of form and matter.[1] Though this terminological denomination is of Aristotelian origin, the central motive designed by it was by no means of Aristotelian invention. It originated from the meeting between two antagonistic Greek religions, namely, the

---

1 For a discussion of the Greek religious basic-motive, see ch. 2, § 7 (a).

older nature religion of life and death, and the younger cultural religion of the Olympian gods. Nietzsche and his friend, Rhode, were the first to discover the conflict between these religions in the Greek tragedies. Nietzsche spoke of the contest between the Dionysian and the Apollinian spirit in these tragedies.[1] But in fact here was at issue a conflict in the religious basic motive of the whole of Greek life and thought.

The pre-Olympian religion of life and death deified the ever-flowing stream of organic life which originates from mother earth and cannot be fixed or restricted by any corporeal form. It is from this formless stream of life that, in the order of time, the generations of beings separate themselves and appear in an individual bodily shape. This corporeal form can only be maintained at the cost of other living beings, so that the life of the one is the death of the other. [163] So there is an injustice in any fixed form of life which for this reason must be repaid to the horrible fate of death, designated by the Greek terms anangke and heimarmene tuche. This is the meaning of the mysterious words of the Ionian philosopher of nature, Anaximander: "The divine origin of all things is the apeiron (i. e., that which lacks a restricting form). The things return to that from which they originate in conformity to the law of justice. For they pay to each other penalty and retribution for their injustice in the order of time."[2] Here the central motive of the archaic religion of life and death has found a clear expression in Anaximander's philosophical view of physis, or nature. It is the motive of the formless stream of life, ever-flowing throughout the process of becoming and passing away, and pertaining to all perishable things which are born in a corporeal form, and subjected to anangke. This is the original sense of the Greek matter-motive. It originated from a deification of the biotic aspect of our temporal horizon of experience and found its most spectacular expression in the cult of Dionysius, imported from Thrace.

b) The form-motive in Greek religion

The religious form-motive, on the other hand, is the central motive of the younger Olympian religion, the religion of form, measure and harmony, wherein the cultural aspect of the Greek polis was deified. It found its most pregnant expression in the Delphian Apollo, the legislator. The Olympian gods are personified cultural powers. They have left mother earth with its ever-flowing stream of life and its ever-threatening [165] fate of death, and have acquired the Olympus as their residence. They have a divine and immortal, personal form, invisible to the eye of sense, an ideal form of a splendid beauty, the genuine prototype of the Platonic notion of the metaphysical eidos, or idea. But these immortal

---

1   See Friedrich Nietzsche, The Birth of Tragedy, in Basic Writings of Nietzsche, ed. Walter Kaufmann (New York: Random House, 1968).
2   Fragment 103A.

gods had no power over the anangke: the fate of death of mortals. This is why the new religion was only accepted as the public religion of the Greek polis. But in their private life, the Greek people held to the old formless deities of life and death, doubtless more crude and incalculable than the Olympians, but more efficient as to the existential needs of man.

Thus the Greek form-matter motive gave expression to a fundamental dualism in the Greek religious consciousness. As the central starting-point of Greek philosophy, it was not dependent upon the mythical forms and representations of the popular belief. By claiming autonomy over against the latter, Greek philosophy certainly did not mean to break with the dualistic basic motive of the Greek religious consciousness. Much rather this motive was the common starting-point of the different philosophical tendencies and schools. But because of its intrinsically dualistic character, it drove Greek philosophical thought into polarly opposed directions. Since a real synthesis between the opposite motives of form and matter was not possible, there remained no other recourse than that of attributing the religious primacy to one of them with the result that the other was depreciated. Whereas in the Ionian nature-philosophy [166] the formless and ever-flowing stream of life was deified, the Aristotelian god is conceived of as pure form whilst the matter-principle is depreciated in the Aristotelian metaphysics as the principle of imperfection.

c) *Dialectical tensions within the Greek religious basic-motive*

In the state of apostasy, the religious impulse, innate in the human heart, turns away from the living God and is directed towards the temporal horizon of human experience with its diversity of modal aspects. This gives rise to the formation of idols which originate from the deification of one of these aspects – that is, in the absolutization of what is only relative. But what is relative can only reveal its meaning in coherence with its correlates. This means that the absolutization of one aspect of our temporal world calls forth, with an inner necessity, correlates of this aspect which now, in the religious consciousness, claim an opposite absoluteness. In other words, every idol gives rise to a counter-idol.

Thus in the Greek religious consciousness the form-motive was bound to the matter-motive as its counterpart. The inner dualism caused in the central starting-point of Greek thought by these two opposite motives gave rise to the dichotomistic view of human nature as a composite of a perishable material body and an immortal, rational soul. It should be noticed that this view originated in the Orphic religious movement. This movement had made the Dionysian religion of life and death into the infra-structure of a higher religion of the celestial sphere, i.e., the starry sky, and interpreted the Olympian religion in this [167] naturalistic sense. In consequence, the central motive of form, measure, and harmony was now transferred to the supra-terrestrial sphere of the starry sky. Man was supposed to have a double origin: his rational soul corresponding to the perfect form and harmony of the starry sphere originates in the latter, but his material body originates from the dark and imperfect sphere of mother earth, with its ever-flowing stream of life and its anangke, its inescapable fate of death. As long as the immortal rational soul is bound to the terrestrial sphere, it is obliged to accept a material body as its prison and grave and it must transmigrate from body to body in the everlasting process of becoming, decline, and rebirth. It is only by means of an ascetic life that the rational soul can purify itself from having been contaminated by the material body, so that at the end of a long period it may return to its proper home, the celestial sphere of form, measure and harmony.

The great influence of this dualistic Orphic view of human nature upon the Pythagorean school, Empedocles, Parmenides, and Plato, is generally known. Since Parmenides, the founder of Greek metaphysics, this dichotomist view was combined with the metaphysical opposition between the realm of eternal being, presenting itself in the ideal spherical form of the heaven, and the phenomenal terrestrial world of coming to be and passing away, subjected to the anangke. Plato purified his metaphysics from Parmenides' naturalistic conception of form. He conceived the eternal forms of being as eide, or ideas. In Plato's dialogue, Phaedo, the proof of the immortality of the rational soul is consequently unbreakably bound to the metaphysical doctrine of the eternal ideas as the ideal forms of being. The latter are sharply opposed to the visible world subjected as it is to the matter-principle of becoming and decay. It was supposed that the metaphysical forms of being are only accessible to logico-theoretical thought, viewed as the center of the immortal soul. The logical function of theoretical thought was considered to be completely independent of the material body since it is focussed upon the eternal forms of being and must consequently be of the same nature as these imperishable forms. Henceforth, the thesis that the logical function of the theoretical act of thought is independent of the material body became a steady argument in the metaphysical proof of the immortality of the soul.

But this argument originated in an absolutization of the antithetical relation which is characteristic of the theoretical attitude of thought. We have seen that in this theoretical attitude the logical aspect of our thought is opposed to the non-logical aspects of experience in order to make the latter accessible to a conceptual analysis. In this way we can make the non-logical aspects of our body into the object of our logico-theoretical inquiry. But we have also established that this antithetical relation between the logical and the non-logical aspects of our temporal experiential horizon does not correspond to reality. It is only the result of a theoretical abstraction of our logical aspect of thought from its unbreakable bond [169] of coherence with all the other aspects of our experience. Under the influence of the dualistic religious form-matter motive, however, Greek metaphysics ascribed to this merely theoretical opposition a metaphysical significance, to the effect that the logico-theoretical function of thought was viewed as an independent substance. In this way there arose the idol of the immortal and rational human soul which was equated with the logical function of our act of theoretical thought. Again in Plato's dialogue, Phaedo, this equation is clearly proclaimed. But it should be noticed that it dated from the first appearance in Greek philosophy of the metaphysical opposition between the eternal form of being and the material world of coming into being and passing away. It was the founder of Greek metaphysics, Parmenides, who was the first to identify theoretical thought with eternal being. In a later phase of his thought, Plato replaced his original view of the simplicity of the human soul by the conception that this soul is composed of two mortal material parts and an immortal spiritual one; nevertheless, he maintained the identification of the latter with the logico-theoretical function of thought. According to him, the latter is the pure form of the soul, viewed apart from its incarnation in the impure material body.

Aristotle, who initially completely accepted both Plato's doctrine of ideas and his dualistic view of soul and body, tried later on to overcome this dualism. He abandoned the separation between the [170] world of the ideal forms and the visible world of perishable material things. He made the ideal form into the immanent principles of being in the perishable substances, which were according to him composed of matter and form. He sought to overcome the central conflict between the matter-motive and the form-motive in the Greek religious consciousness by reducing it to the complementary relation of a material and a form given to it, in the sense in which the relation is found in the cultural aspect of experience. As the principle of coming into being and passing away, matter has, according to him, no actual but only potential being. It is only by a substantial form that it can have actual existence. Form and matter are united in the natural things into one natural substance, and this natural substance would be the absolute reference point of all properties we ascribe to the thing.

This metaphysical view was also applied to man as a natural substance. Thus the rational soul was conceived of as the substantial form of the perishable material body. Since, however, the soul is only the substantial form of the body without being itself a substance, it cannot exist apart from the material body and lacks, in consequence, immortality. What, according to Aristotle, is really an immortal substance is only the active theoretical intellect which, in his opinion, does not stem from human nature, but comes from the outside into the soul.[1] This active theoretical thought, however, lacks any individuality, since individuality stems from matter, and active theoretical [171] thought remains completely separated from the material body. It is the pure and actual form of thinking, and as such, it has a general character. Here the fundamental dualism in the form-matter motive, which at first sight seemed to be overcome by Aristotle, clearly reappears. In fact, it could not be overcome since it ruled the central starting-point of Greek philosophical thought.

§ 26. The scholastic appropriation of the Greek basic-motive

Thomas Aquinas tried to accommodate the Aristotelian view of human nature to the doctrine of the Church. First, he adapted it to the doctrine of divine creation, which, as such, was incompatible with the Greek form-matter motive. According to Thomas, God created man as a natural substance composed of matter and form.[2] Second, he interpreted the Aristotelian view in such a way that the rational soul was conceived of both as the form of the material body and as an immortal substance which can exist apart from the body.[3] He accepted the Aristotelian view that matter contains the principle of individuation and that form as such lacks individuality. The Aristotelian view that the active theoretical intellect does not originate from the natural process of development but comes from the outside, was interpreted in a so-called psycho-creationist sense: God creates every immortal rational soul apart. But the result of this scholastic accommodation was a complex of insoluble contradictions.

In the first place, the psycho-creationist doctrine contradicts the emphatic biblical statement (Genesis 2:2) that God had finished all his works of creation. [172] Thus a whole complex of theological pseudo-problems was introduced. If God continues to create rational souls after the fall of man, does he create sinful souls, or should we assume that sin originates only from the material body? The traditional solution of this problem to the effect that God creates souls deprived of the original state of communion with him, but not sinful in themselves, is unbiblical to such a degree that it does not need any further argumentation. For what else is the fall into sin than breaking the communion with God, i. e., what else than the state of apostasy from him? Secondly, if the im-

---

1 De Anima, III.5.
2 Summa Theologiae, Ia.75.4.
3 ST, Ia.75.6, 76.1.

mortal soul is individualized only by the material body, how can it re-
tain its individuality after its separation from the body?

I shall not go into a more detailed discussion of these scholastic problems.[1] The vitium originis of this psycho-creationist theory is its un-
biblical starting-point, which cannot be made innocuous by any scholastic accommodation to the Church's doctrine and by an appeal to texts of
Scripture. For the theological exegesis of these texts is in this case itself
infected by this un-biblical starting-point. It lacks the key of knowledge
which alone can open to us the radical sense of the divine Word-
revelation. For let me end this latest lecture with words of Calvin in the
beginning of the first chapter of his Institutio Religiionis Christianae,
"The true knowledge of ourselves is dependent upon the true knowledge
of God" (I.i.1).

---

1   For Dooyeweerd's extensive discussion of these themes, see his three-volume work,
    Reformation and Scholasticism in Philosophy, Collected Works, Series A, Volumes
    5-7.

PART FOUR

Towards a Radically Biblical Anthropology

Chapter Eight

What is Man?

§ 27. The crisis of Western civilization and the twilight of western thought

The question, "What is man?"[1] occupies a central place in contemporary European thinking. This question is certainly not new. After every period in the history of Western thought wherein all interest was concentrated upon the knowledge of the outer world, i.e. the immense universe, man began to feel unsatisfied. In this situation human reflection always turns again to the central riddle of man's own existence. As soon as this riddle begins to puzzle human thought, it seems as if the external world recedes from the focus of interest. In one of his splendid dialogues, Plato pictures his master, Socrates, as a man obsessed with but one aim in his search for wisdom, namely, to know himself.[2] As long as I have not succeeded in learning to know myself, said Socrates, I have no time for meddling with other questions that seem to me trifles when compared with this.

In contemporary European thinking, however, the question, "What is man?," is no longer asked from a theoretical viewpoint only. Much rather it has become a crucial issue for many thinkers because of the spiritual distress of Western society and the fundamental [174] crisis of our culture. It may be that in America this crisis does not occupy the same central place in the reflection of the leading thinkers as it does in

---

1   As noted in the Concluding Remarks, because In Twilight is very much a historically-located text (and originally published in English), the language of the original text has been retained. Of course, we would today ask – as Dooyeweerd was indeed asking in the language of his time – "What is the human person?" In a recent essay, Janet Wesselius enlists Dooyeweerd in the project of a feminist critique of modern conceptions of the subject, drawing on Dooyeweerd's anthropology. See Janet Catherina Wesselius, "Points of Convergence Between Dooyeweerdian and Feminist Views of the Philosophic Self," in James H. Olthuis, ed., Knowing Other-wise: Philosophy on the Threshold of Spirituality, Perspectives in Continental Philosophy (Bronx, NY: Fordham University Press, 1997), pp. 54-68.

2   The maxim, "Know thyself," was given to Socrates by the Oracle at Delphi (Xenophon, Memorabilia, IV.2.24-25).

Europe. Nevertheless, America too is concerned with the same problem, since it belongs to the sphere of Western civilization.

What then is the nature of this crisis? And why does the question, "What is man?" today sound like a cry of distress? The crisis of Western civilization is depicted as a complete decline of human personality and the rise of mass-man. This is attributed by different leading thinkers to the increasing supremacy of technology and to the over-organization of modern society.[1] The result, it is thought, is a process of the depersonalization of contemporary life. Modern mass-man has lost all personal traits: his pattern of behavior is prescribed by what is done in general; he shifts the responsibility for his behavior upon an impersonal society. And this society, in turn, seems to be ruled by the robot, the electronic brain, by bureaucracy, fashion, organization and other impersonal powers. As a result, our contemporary society has no room for human personality and a real spiritual person-to-person communion. Even the family and the church can often no longer guarantee a sphere of personal interchange and dialogue. Family life is, to a large degree, dislocated by increasing industrialization. The church itself is confronted with the danger of the depersonalization of congregational life, especially in the big cities.

In addition, the average secularized man nowadays [175] has lost any and all true interest in religion. He has fallen prey to a state of spiritual nihilism; that is, he negates all spiritual values. He has lost all his faith and denies any higher ideals than the satisfaction of his desires. Even the Humanistic faith in mankind and in the power of human reason to rule the world and elevate man to a higher level of freedom and morality no longer has any appeal to the mind of the present day mass-man. To him God is dead; and the two World Wars have destroyed the Humanistic ideal of man. Modern mass-man has lost himself, and considers himself cast into a world that is meaningless, that offers no hope for a better future.

Western civilization, which displays these terrible symptoms of spiritual decline, finds itself confronted with the totalitarian ideology of Communism. It tries to oppose the latter with the old ideas of democracy, freedom, and of inalienable human rights. But these ideas too have been involved in the spiritual crisis which has sapped their very fundamentals. In earlier times, it is argued, they were rooted both in the Christian faith and in the Humanists' faith in reason. But the increasing relativism, which has affected our Western civilization, has left no room for a strong faith since it has destroyed the belief in an absolute truth.

---

1 Cp. Heidegger's analysis of the 'they' (das Man) and its relation to an industrial, technological society. See Heidegger, Being and Time, trans. John Macquarrie and Edward Robinson (New York: Harper & Row, 1962), § 27.

The traditional faith which gave man his inspiration, has to a great extent been replaced by technical methods and organization. And in general it is because of such impersonal means that the traditional Christian and Humanistic traits of our culture are being outwardly maintained.

But Western civilization cannot be saved by technical [176] and organizational means alone. The Communist world-power, whose ideology is still rooted in a strong faith, also has these means at its disposal and has used them very well. Besides, the atom bomb which terminated the Second World War is no longer an American monopoly. This terrible invention of Western technology can only increase the fear of the impending ruin of our culture. The amazing technical development of Western society, which has produced modern mass-man, will also destroy our civilization unless a way is found to restore human personality.

§ 28. Existentialist philosophy as a response to the crisis

It is against this background of spiritual distress that the question: "What is man?" has become truly existential in contemporary European philosophy. It is no longer merely a question of theoretical interest. It has become, rather, a question concerning the whole existence of man in his spiritual anxiety. It is a question of 'to be or not to be.' This also explains the powerful influence of contemporary personalistic and existentialist philosophical trends on European literature and on young people.[1] Here it is no longer an abstract idealistic image of man as a rational and moral being which is at issue; rather, the new philosophical view of man is concerned with man in his concrete situation in the world, with his state of decay as the contemporary mass-man, and with his possibilities of rediscovering himself as a responsible personality.

This philosophy no longer considers the intellect as the real center of human nature.[2] It has tried to penetrate, instead, to what is conceived to be the deepest root of human self-hood and the deepest [177] cause of man's spiritual distress: man is thrown into the world involuntarily.[3] To sustain his life he is obliged to turn to the things that are at hand in his world. The struggle for existence characterizes man's life; but in this

---

1 Principally the influence of authors such as Heidegger, Sartre, Camus, and Beckett.

2 In its displacement of rationalism and the dominant traditional interpretation of the human person as a 'rational animal,' existentialism is an ally in Dooyeweerd's project, which seeks to emphasize the multi-dimensionality of the human person. (The problem with existentialism, as Dooyeweerd sees it, is that it fails to recognize the transcendence of the self and its meaning in relation to its Origin.) What follows in this paragraph is a sketch of the main themes of Heidegger's Being and Time.

3 On 'throwness' (Geworfenheit), see Heidegger, Being and Time, § 38.

situation of concern[1] man is in danger of losing himself as a free personality so that he delivers himself to the world – for the human selfhood surpasses all existing things. The human ego is free. It is not at-hand as a concrete object; it is able to project its own future and to say to its past, "I am no longer what I was yesterday. My future is still in my own hand. I can change myself. I can create my future by my own power." But, this philosophy goes on, when man reflects on this creative freedom of his selfhood, he is confronted with the deepest cause of his distress, namely, the anxiety and fear of death.[2] Death, it holds, is here not understood in the merely biological sense in which it also applies to the animal, but much rather in the sense of the dark nothingness, the night without dawn, which puts an end to all human projects and makes them meaningless. This anxiety, this fear of death is usually suppressed, for such is mass-man's depersonalized manner of existence. To arrive at a proper personal existence, man should frankly and in anticipation confront himself with death as the nothingness which limits his freedom. He should realize that his freedom is a freedom unto death, ending in the dark nothingness. Thus did this first existentialist approach to human self-knowledge reveal ts so profoundly pessimistic view of man.

However, other existentialist thinkers showed a [178] more hopeful possibility of rediscovering man's true personality. In accordance with the personalistic philosophy of Martin Buber,[3] they pointed to the essential communal relation in our personal life. You and I are correlates, who presuppose each other, they reasoned. I cannot know myself without taking into account that my ego is related to the ego of my fellowman. And I cannot really have a personal meeting with another ego without love. It is only by such a meeting in love that I can arrive at true self-knowledge and knowledge of my fellow-man.

In this way this philosophy, then, seemed to offer various perspectives for a more profound knowledge of man's selfhood. And there are also many theologians who are of the opinion that this existentialist approach to the central problem of man's nature and destiny is of a more biblical character than the traditional theological view of human nature, oriented to ancient Greek philosophy. I fear that this theological opinion testifies to a lack of self-knowledge in its radical biblical sense. It will presently become apparent why I think so. However, let us first establish that the whole preceding diagnosis of the spiritual crisis of Western civilization fails to lay bare the root of the evil. For the symptoms of the spiritual decadence of this civilization that are manifesting themselves in an increasing expansion of the nihilistic mind cannot be explained by

1 On 'concern' (besorgen) and 'care' (Sorge), see Being and Time, §§ 41-43.

2 On 'Being-towards-death,' see Being and Time, §§50-53.

3 Cp. the earlier discussion of Buber , ch. 2, § 5.

external causes. They are only the ultimate result of a religious process of apostasy, which started with the belief in [179] the absolute self-sufficiency of the rational human personality and was doomed to end with the breaking down of this idol.

§ 29. The meaning of the self

a) *The transcendence of the self*

How, then, can we arrive at real self-knowledge? The question, "Who is man?" contains a mystery that cannot be explained by man himself.

In the last century, when the belief in so-called objective science was still predominant in the leading circles, it was supposed that by continued empirical research science would succeed in solving all the problems of human existence. Now there is undoubtedly a scientific way of acquiring knowledge about human existence. There are many special sciences which are concerned with the study of man; but each of them considers human life only from a particular viewpoint or aspect. Physics and chemistry, biology, psychology, historiography, sociology, jurisprudence, ethics, and so forth, all furnish interesting information about man. But when one asks them: "What is man himself, in the central unity of his existence, in his selfhood?" then these sciences have no answer. The reason is that they are bound to the temporal order of our experience. Within this temporal order human existence presents a great diversity of aspects, just like the whole temporal world in which man finds himself placed. Physics and chemistry inform us about the material constellation of the human body and the electro-magnetic forces operating in it; biology lays bare the functions of our organic life; psychology gives us an insight into the emotional life of feeling and will and has even penetrated to the unconscious [180] sphere of our mind. History informs us about the development of human culture, linguistics about the human faculty of expressing thoughts and feelings by means of words and other symbolical signs; economics and jurisprudence study the economic and juridical aspects of human social life, and so forth. Thus every special science studies temporal human existence in one of its different aspects.

But all these aspects of our experience and existence within the order of time are related to the central unity of our consciousness which we call our I, our ego. I experience, I exist, and this I surpasses the diversity of aspects which human life displays within the temporal order. The ego cannot be determined by any aspect of our temporal experience since it is the central reference point of all of them. If man should lack this central I, he could not have any experience at all.

b) A critique of existentialism

Consequently, contemporary existentialist philosophy has rightly posited that it is not possible to acquire real self-knowledge by means of scientific research. But it pretens that its own philosophical approach to human existence does lead us to this self-knowledge. Science, it says, is restricted to the investigation of what is given, to concrete objects at hand. But, it argues, the human ego is not a given object. It has the freedom to create itself by contriving its own future. Thus existentialist philosophy pretends that it is specifically directed towards discovering this freedom of the human I in the face of all that can be seen in the world to the contrary.

But that we can arrive at real self-knowledge in this way? Can this philosophy actually penetrate to the real center and root of our existence, as many contemporary theologians think? I am of the opinion that it is a vain illusion to think so. Philosophical thought is bound to the temporal order of human experience, just as the special sciences are. Within this temporal order, man's existence presents itself only in a rich diversity of aspects, but not in that radical and central unity which we call our I or selfhood. It is true that our temporal existence presents itself as an individual bodily whole and that its different aspects are related to this whole – and are, in fact, only aspects of it. But, as a merely temporal wholeness, our human existence does not display that central unity which we are aware of in our self-consciousness. This central I, which surpasses the temporal order, remains a veritable mystery.[1] As soon as we try to grasp it in a concept or definition, it recedes as a phantom and resolves itself into nothingness. Is it really a nothing, as some philosophers have said? The mystery of the human I is that it is, indeed, nothing in itself; that is to say, it is nothing as long as we try to conceive it apart from the three central relations which alone give it meaning.[2]

First, our human ego is related to our whole temporal existence and to our entire experience of the temporal world as the central reference point of the latter. Second, it finds itself, indeed, in an essential communal relation to the egos of its fellowmen. [182] Third, it points beyond itself to its central relation to its divine Origin in Whose image man was created. The first relation, namely, that of the human ego to the temporal order of the world in which we are placed, cannot lead us to real

1 Blaise Pascal, following Augustine, points to the enigma or mystery of the self: "Man is beyond man. [...] Be aware, then, proud men, what a paradox you are to yourselves! Humble yourself, powerless reason! Be silent, foolish nature! Learn that humanity infinitely transcends humanity and hear from your Master your true condition of which you are unaware." Pascal, Pensées, trans. Honor Levi (Oxford: Oxford University Press, 1995), § 164.

2 The discussion that follows parallels the development in ch. 2, §§ 4-6.

self-knowledge so long as it is viewed in itself alone. The temporal order of human life in the world, with its diversity of aspects, can only
turn away our view from the real center of human existence so long as
we seek to know ourselves from it. Shall we seek our selfhood in the
spatial aspect of our temporal existence, or in the physico-chemical aspect of the material constellation of our body, or in the aspect of its organic life, or in that of emotional feeling? Or should we rather identify
our ego with the logical aspect of our thought, or with the historical aspect of our cultural life in a temporal society, or with the aesthetical, or
the moral aspect of our temporal existence? By so doing we would lose
sight of the real center and radical unity of our human nature. The temporal order of our experiential world is like a prism which refracts or
disperses the sun-light into a rich diversity of colors; none of these colors is the light itself. In the same way the central human ego is not to be
determined by any of the different aspects of our temporal, earthly existence.

The second relation in which our selfhood is to be conceived is the
communal relation of our own ego to that of our fellow-man. This relation can no more lead us to real self-knowledge than can the relation of
our ego to the temporal world as long as it is viewed in itself alone. The
reason is that the ego of [183] our fellow-man confronts us with the
same riddle as our own selfhood does. So long as we try to understand
the relation between you and me merely from the temporal order of this
earthly human existence, we must posit that this relation presents the
same diversity of aspects as our own temporal existence. Whether we
conceive of it in its moral, psychological, historico-cultural or biological
aspect, we will not arrive at any knowledge of the central relationship
between your and mine. By so doing we only lose sight of its central
character, which surpasses the diversity of aspects in our temporal horizon of existence.

The personalistic and existentialist views of man have tried to determine the I-thou relation as a relation of love, an inner meeting of the human persons. But within the earthly horizon of time, even the love relations present a diversity of meaning and typical character. Does one refer to the love between husband and wife, or between parents and their
children? Or is it the love-relation between fellow-believers, belonging
to inter-related churches, that we have in mind? Or is it perhaps the
love-relation between compatriots who have in common the love of
their country? Or have we rather in mind the general love of the neighbor in the moral relations of our temporal life? None of these temporal
communal relations touch the central sphere of our selfhood. And when
contemporary philosophy speaks of an inner meeting of the one person
with the other, we must ask, "What do you understand by this inner
[184] meeting?" A real inner meeting presupposes real self-knowledge
and can only occur in the central religious sphere of our relation with

our fellow-man. The temporal love-relations, in the above mentioned typical diversity of meaning, cannot guarantee a true inner meeting. Jesus said in the Sermon on the Mount, "if you love them who love you, what thanks do you have? For sinners also love those that love them" (Luke 6:32). Jesus here apparently speaks of a love that does not concern the real center of our lives, but only the temporal relations between men in their earthly diversity. How then can we love our enemies and bless those who curse us, and pray for those who persecute us, if we do not love God in Jesus Christ?

c) The meaning of the self in its religious relation to the Origin

Therefore, the inter-personal relation between you and me cannot lead us to real self-knowledge as long as it is not conceived in its central sense; and in this central sense it points beyond itself to the ultimate relation between the human I and God. This latter central relation is of a religious character. No philosophical reflection can lead us to real self-knowledge in a purely philosophical way. The words with which Calvin starts the first chapter of his text-book on the Christian religion – "The true knowledge of ourselves is dependent on the true knowledge of God" (Institutes I.i.1) – are indeed the key to answer the question: "Who is man himself?"

But if that is so, it seems that we should look to theology for real self-knowledge since theology seems to be specifically concerned with the knowledge of God. However, this too would amount to self-deceit. For as a dogmatical[1] [185] science of the articles of the Christian faith, theology is no more able to lead us to real knowledge of ourselves and of God than philosophy or the special sciences which are concerned with the study of man.[2] This central knowledge can only be the result of the Word-revelation of God operating in the heart, in the religious center of our existence by the power of the Holy Spirit. Jesus Christ never blamed the scribes and Pharisees for a lack of dogmatical theological knowledge. When Herod asked the Chief priest and scribes where Christ was to be born, he received an answer that was undoubtedly correct from a dogmatical theological view-point since it was based upon the prophetical texts of the Old Testament. Nevertheless, Jesus said that they did not know Him nor his Father (John 5). And how could they have had real self-knowledge without this knowledge of God in Jesus Christ?

---

1 'Dogmatical' not in the sense of rigid or inflexible, but rather as a science of dogma, the teachings of the church.

2 Recall Dooyeweerd's careful distinction between theology as a theoretical science of the faith aspect, and religion as the commitment of the heart, worked out in chapter six.

The traditional theological view of man, which we find both in Roman Catholic and Protestant scholastic works on dogmatics, was not at all of a biblical origin.[1] According to this theological conception of human nature, man is composed of a mortal, material body and of an immaterial, rational soul. These components were conceived of as united to one substance. Nevertheless, according to this view, the rational soul continues to exist as an independent substance after the separation from the body, i. e., after death. In line with this view of human nature, man was called a rational and moral being in contrast to the animal which lacks a rational soul. This view of man was, indeed, taken from Greek [186] philosophy, which sought the center of our human existence in reason; that is, in the intellect.

But in this entire image of man there was no room for the real – that is, the religious center of our existence which in the Holy Scripture is called our heart, the spiritual root of all the temporal manifestations of our life. It was constructed apart from the central theme of the Word-revelation, that of creation, fall into sin, and redemption by Jesus Christ in the communion of the Holy Spirit. And yet it is this very core of the divine Revelation that alone reveals the true root and center of human life. It is the only key to true self-knowledge in its dependency on the true knowledge of God. It is also the only judge both of all theological and philosophical views of man. As such, this central theme of the Word-revelation cannot be dependent on theological interpretations and conceptions, which are fallible human work, bound to the temporal order of our existence and experience. Its radical sense can only be explained by the Holy Spirit who opens our hearts so that our belief is no longer a mere acceptance of the articles of the Christian faith but a living belief, instrumental to the central operation of God's Word in the heart, namely, the religious center of our lives. And this operation does not occur in an individualistic way, but in the ecumenical communion of the Holy Spirit who unites all the members of the true Catholic Church in its spiritual sense, irrespective of their temporal denominational divisions.

§ 30. Word-revelation and the biblical basic-motive

a) The theme of revelation: creation, fall, and redemption

Naturally, creation, the fall into sin and the redemption through Jesus Christ as the Incarnate Word [187] in the communion of the Holy Spirit are also articles of faith, which are dealt with in every theological dogmatics in addition to other articles which too are, actually or supposedly founded in the Holy Scriptures. But in their radical sense as the central theme of the Word-revelation and the key of knowledge, they are not merely articles of faith which are only human formulations of the con-

---

1   The following echoes the themes developed in more detail in chapter seven.

fession of the Church; much rather, they are the Word of God itself in its central spiritual power addressing itself to the heart, the religious core and center of our existence. In this central confrontation with the Word of God, man has nothing to give but only needs to listen and to receive. God does not speak to theologians, philosophers and scientists, but to sinners, lost in themselves, and made into his children through the operation of the Holy Spirit in their hearts. In this central and radical sense, God's Word, penetrating to the root of our being, has to become the central motive-power of all of Christian life within the temporal order with its rich diversity of aspects, occupational spheres and tasks.[1] As such, the central theme of creation, fall into sin and redemption, should also be the central starting-point and motive power of our theological and philosophical thought.

Is it necessary at this point to consider the radical meaning of this central theme of the divine Word-revelation? Is it not rather well known to all of us since the beginning of our Christian education? [Yes, but then again] it may well be questioned whether this is really true. I am afraid that for many Christians who do have a [188] theological knowledge of creation, fall into sin an redemption by Jesus Christ, this central theme of the Word-revelation has not yet become the central motive-power of their lives.

b) The radical sense of creation, fall, and redemption

What is the radical, biblical sense of the revelation of creation? As Creator, God reveals himself as the absolute Origin of all that exists outside of himself. There is no power in the world that is independent of him. Even Satan is a creature and his power is taken from creation, namely, from the creation of man in the image of God.[2] If man had not been created in God's image, Satan's suggestion that man would be like God (Gen. 3:5) would have had no single power over the human heart. He could only give this power an apostate direction, but his power does not originate from himself. If our heart finds itself fully in the grip of the self-revelation of God as Creator, we can no longer imagine that there would exist a safe and neutral zone which is withdrawn from God. This is the fundamental difference between the living God and the idols

---

1 Here and in what follows, Dooyeweerd echoes the themes of his mentor, Abraham Kuyper, – namely, the lordship of Christ over all of life such that there is no sphere concerning which Christ cannot say, "Mine!" "In fact," Kuyper remarked in a dedicatory speech at the Free University of Amsterdam, "there is not to be a fingerprint speck of territory in our whole human life about which the Christ, who is sovereign over everything, is not calling out, 'That belongs to me!'" (Kuyper, Souvereiniteit in eigen kring [Amsterdam: Kruyt, 1880]: 35, as translated by Calvin Seerveld). Thus, a radical or integral understanding of creation, fall, and redemption will reflect itself in every facet of life: theory, occupations, family, etc.

2 Augustine, De Vera Religione, xiii.26.

which originate from an absolutization of what has only a relative and dependent existence. The ancient Greeks, whose conception of human nature had such a predominant influence upon the traditional theological view of man, worshipped their Olympian gods who were merely deified cultural powers of Greek society. These gods were represented as invisible and immortal beings endowed with a splendid beauty and a suprahuman power. But these splendid gods had no power over the fate of death to which mortals are subjected. This is why the famous Greek poet, Homer, said: "Even the immortal gods cannot help lamentable man, when the horrible fate of death strikes him down." And the same poet says that the immortal gods fight shy of every contact with the realm of death.

But hear now what Psalm 139 says about God: "Whither shall I go from thy Spirit? Or whither shall I flee from thy presence? If I ascend up into heaven, thou art there: If I make my bed in the realm of death, behold, thou art there" (vv. 7-8). Here we face the living God as Creator, whom the ancient Greeks did not know. In an indissoluble contact with this self-revelation as Creator, God has revealed man to himself. Man was created in the image of God. Just as God is the absolute Origin of all that exists outside of himself, so he created man as a being in whom the entire diversity of aspects and faculties of the temporal world is concentrated within the religious center of his existence, which we call our I, and which the Holy Scripture calls our heart,[1] in a pregnant, religious sense. As the central seat of the image of God, the human selfhood was endowed with the innate religious impulse to concentrate its whole temporal life and the whole temporal world upon the service of love to God. And since the love for God implies the love for his image in man, the whole diversity of God's temporal ordinances is related to the central, religious commandment of love, namely, "thou shalt love the Lord, thy God, with all thy heart, soul and mind, and thy neighbor as thyself" (Mark 12:30-31). This is the radical [190] biblical sense of the creation of man in the image of God. It leaves no room for any neutral sphere in life which could be withdrawn from the central commandment in the kingdom of God.

Since the image of God in man concerned the radix, that is, the religious center and root of our entire temporal existence, it follows that the fall into sin can only be understood in the same radical, biblical sense. The whole fall into sin can be summarized as being the vain illusion that arose in the human heart, namely, that the human I has the same absolute existence as God himself. This was the false insinuation of Satan, to which man gave ear: "Ye shall be like God." This apostasy from the living God implied the spiritual death of man, since the human I is nothing

1   See, for example, Genesis 8:21; 1 Kings 15:3; Psalm 51:10; Jeremiah 17:9-10; Matthew 6:21; Mark 12:30; Romans 10:10.

in itself and can only live from the Word of God and in the love-communion with its divine Creator. However this original sin could not destroy the religious center of human existence with its innate religious impulse to seek for its absolute Origin. It could only lead the central impulsion in a false, apostate direction by diverting it to the temporal world with its rich diversity of aspects, which, however, have only a relative sense.

By seeking his God and himself in the temporal world, and by elevating a relative and dependent aspect of this world to the rank of the absolute, man fell prey to idolatry: he lost the true knowledge of God and true self-knowledge. The idea that true self-knowledge may be regained by an existentialist philosophy, apart from the divine Word-revelation, [191] is nothing but the old vain illusion that the human I is something in itself, independent of God who has revealed himself as the Creator. It is only in Jesus Christ, the incarnate Word and Redeemer, that the image of God has been restored in the religious center of human nature. The redemption by Jesus Christ in its radical biblical sense means the rebirth of our heart. It must reveal itself in the whole of our temporal life. Consequently, there now can be no real self-knowledge apart from Jesus Christ. And this biblical self-knowledge implies that our whole world-and-life-view must be reformed in a Christo-centric sense, so that every dualistic view of common grace which separates the latter from its true religious root and center in Jesus Christ should be rejected in principle.

The history of dogmatic theology proves that it is possible to give a seemingly orthodox theoretical explanation of the articles of faith pertaining to the threefold central theme of Holy Scripture without any awareness of the central and radical significance of the latter for the view of human nature and of the temporal world. When that occurs, theological thought does not really find itself in the grip of the Word of God insofar as the latter has not become its central basic-motive, its central impelling force. Rather, it proves itself to be influenced by another, non-biblical central motive which gives to it its ultimate direction. Such was the scholastic theme of nature and grace (introduced into Roman Catholic theology and philosophy since the 13th century) which ruled the traditional [192] theological view of man. It led scholastic theology to divide human life into two spheres, namely, the natural and the supra-natural. Human nature was supposed to belong to the natural sphere, and was supposed to find its center in natural reason. Human reason would be able to acquire a correct insight into human nature, and into all other so-called natural truths, apart from any divine Revelation, by its own natural light alone. Of course, it was granted that this rational nature of man was created by God; but this theological acceptance of creation as revealed truth did not influence the view of human nature it-self. This view was instead ruled to a far greater extent by the dualistic pagan religious basic motive of Greek thought, which in turn led to a so-called dichotomist conception of the nature of man.

In addition to his rational-ethical nature, man was supposed to have been endowed with a supernatural gift of grace, namely, participation in the divine nature. According to Roman Catholic doctrine this su-pra-natural gift of grace was lost by the fall into sin; and is regained by the supra-natural means of grace, which Christ has entrusted to his Church. In this way, the human rational nature would be elevated to that supra-natural state of perfection to which it was destined in accordance with the plan of creation. It was granted, however, that man cannot ar-rive at this state without faith, which is itself a gift of grace to the hu-man intellect; and it is, therefore, only by faith that we can accept the supra-natural truths of divine Revelation. But the supra-natural sphere of grace presupposes the natural [193] sphere of human life, namely, human nature. This nature, according to the Roman Catholic view, was not radically corrupted by sin; it was only wounded, since, in accor-dance with the plan of creation, it was destined to be united with the su-pra-natural gift of grace. As a result of original sin, human nature lost its original harmony. The sensuous inclinations are in opposition to natural reason which should rule over them. Nevertheless, man can arrive on his own at the acquisition of natural virtues by which the rule of reason over the sensuous inclinations is realized. So, it maintains, only the su-pra-natural virtues of faith, hope and Christian love belong to the sphere of grace.[1]

That is the view of human nature which has been sanctioned by the doctrine of the Roman Catholic Church. It has completely abandoned the radical sense of creation, fall and redemption, as they are revealed to us in the Word of God. The Roman Catholic view of this central theme of Revelation was rejected by the Reformation. But how is it to be ex-plained that the conception of human nature as a composite of a material body and an immortal, rational soul was, nevertheless, generally ac-cepted by both scholastic Lutheran and Reformed theology. Was this conception not taken from Greek philosophy, whose pagan religious ba-sic motive was radically opposed to that of Holy Scripture? Did this Ro-man Catholic dualism not fail to take account of the biblical insight into the religious root and center of human existence? Was it not, conse-quently, incompatible with the biblical doctrine concerning the radical [194] character of the fall into sin, which affected human nature in its very root? How, then, could this un-biblical view of man be main-tained? The reason is that the scholastic basic motive of nature and

---

1 On the 'natural' virtues, see Aquinas, Summa Theologiae, IaIIae.55.1; on the 'theo-logical' virtues, see qu. 62.

grace of Roman Catholicism continued to influence the theological and philosophical views of the Reformation. This motive introduced a dualism into the entire view of man and the world which could not fail to draw Christian thought away from the radical and integral grip of the Word of God. It is this very dualism which testifies to its un-biblical character: it was the result of the attempt to accommodate the Greek view of nature to the biblical doctrine of grace. In fact, this scholastic motive of accommodation resulted in a radical deformation of the central theme of the Word-revelation. The scholastic view, i.e. that created human nature finds its center in an autonomous human reason, cannot be accommodated to the radical biblical view of creation because it implies that, in the 'natural' sphere of life, man would be independent of the Word of God. This false division of human life into a natural and a supra-natural sphere became the starting-point of the process of secularization, which subsequently resulted in the crisis of Western culture in its spiritual uprooting. In fact, it abandoned the so-called natural sphere to the rule of the apostate religious basic motive, initially to that of Greek thought, later on to that of modern Humanism.

Human reason is not an independent substance. Rather it is an instrument. And the I is the concealed player who avails himself of it.

Furthermore, the central motive that rules both human thought and the human ego itself is of a central religious nature. The question: "What is man? Who is he?", cannot be answered by man himself. However, it has been answered by God's Word-revelation, which uncovers the religious root and center of human nature in its creation, fall into sin and redemption by Jesus Christ. Man lost true self-knowledge when he lost the true knowledge of God. But all idols of the human selfhood, which man in his apostasy has devised, break down when they are confronted with the Word of God which unmasks their vanity and nothingness. It is this Word alone which, by its radical grip, can bring about a real reformation of our view of man and of our view of the temporal world; and such an inner reformation is the very opposite of the scholastic device of accommodation.

Concluding Remarks
and Acknowledgements

The preparation of this edition of In the Twilight of Western Thought for Dooyeweerd's Collected Works involved the following editorial tasks:

1. Unlike many of the other works in the Collected Works, the original text of this particular volume was written and published in English from the outset (see my discussion of the text in the Editor's Introduction); therefore, there was no need for translation as such in this case. This edition closely tracks the original text which was first published in 1960 by the Presbyterian and Reformed Publishing House in Philadelphia and was subsequently reprinted in 1968 by the Craig Press of Nutley, N.J. For this edition I retained virtually all the original language of the text notwithstanding its drawbacks, particularly with regard to gender-exclusive language and other sometimes rather unusual phraseology resulting from Dooyeweerd's less than fluent knowledge of the English language. However, I did make certain mostly minor changes as explained below.

   This being a historically situated and already previously published original text, I did not feel free to alter the text in any significant way to conform to contemporary practice and sensibilities. One ought to read this as we read Plato, Kant or Hegel, i.e. with attention to the conditions of its original production. The changes I did make include minor corrections of spelling and grammar, as well as some changes in punctuation, particularly the elimination of gratuitous commas. In addition, in consultation with the general editor, I have very selectively employed some alternate wording from time to time to improve the readability and flow where this was feasible without altering in any way the sense of the original text. In view of these changes and to facilitate comparison in case of need, I retained the pagination numbers of the original 1960 (and 1968 reprinted) editions in square brackets within this revised edition of Dooyeweerd's text.

2. The original edition of the book was published without headings or organizational indicators; it simply included eight chapters, "The Pretended Autonomy of Philosophic Thought," I and II; "The

Sense of History and the Historical World and Life View," I and II, "Philosophy and Theology," I-III, and "What is Man?" For this edition, I divided the text into Four Parts: "The Pretended Autonomy of Philosophic Thought," "Historicism and the Sense of History," "Philosophy and Theology," and "Towards a Radically Biblical Anthropology." Excluding chapter eight, the chapter titles within each of these parts are my own. In addition, I organized the running text by subdividing it into sections (§), of which some are further subdivided. All of these headings are my additions and are intended to indicate the development of the argument and to break up the text into manageable sections, particularly for use in teaching. The Table of Contents gives an overview of this organization.

3. While Dooyeweerd is constantly engaging the history of philosophy in this text, the original edition provided no references. All of the footnotes in this edition are mine, and one of the primary purposes of these notes is to provide references for the thinkers and themes which Dooyeweerd engages. Dooyeweerd makes few direct citations; thus, for many of the references, I simply pointed the reader to texts where the theme is addressed. For instance, when Dooyeweerd discusses Aquinas' understanding of the relationship between nature and grace, a masss of texts from Thomas' corpus could be cited. I have indicated places where the theme is discussed in readily available texts.

For these references, I have tried wherever possible to cite English translations, and in most cases, the standard editions in the field. I would like to thank Dr. Theodore Plantinga for help with a Dilthey reference, and Dr. Micheal Prosch for pointing me to the source of a Hegel citation.

4. In addition to providing references, I have also added notes with three purposes in mind: a) to briefly explain technical terms in Dooyeweerd's thought and point to other places in his corpus where these themes are addressed, particularly for the student first engaging his philosophy; b) to note Dooyeweerd's debts and relationships to the history of philosophy and Christian thought – particularly Augustine and Calvin; c) to indicate Dooyeweerd's relationship to twentieth-century continental philosophy – particularly neo-Kantianism and phenomenology – which functions as the horizon or environment of his work. Where appropriate, I have also referred the reader to the work of contemporary scholars who have critically engaged and appropriated Dooyeweerd's work.

Work on this text was made possible in part by a fellowship from the Social Sciences and Humanities Research Council of Canada, whose support is gratefully acknowledged. I would also like to take the opportunity to thank Dr. Danie Strauss, Director of the Dooyeweerd Centre for Christian Philosophy, for the opportunity to work on this edition of In Twilight. I consider it an honor to have been able to play a role in the publication of this text in the Collected Works. My first reading of this book was during my first week of graduate studies; as a decided (Protestant!) Thomist at the time – a good scholastic, Dooyeweerd would say – I recall returning home in tears one evening precisely because of the challenge of the book. In Twilight was the pivotal book in my career, and I am delighted to be able to show my gratitude to it – and Prof. Dooyeweerd – by preparing this edition, which I hope will confront and challenge many more students.

I would like to dedicate this edition to my first teachers who introduced me to Dooyeweerd: Dr. Robert Sweetman and Dr. Hendrik Hart, both of the Institute for Christian Studies. I only hope that I have carried on the task of radical Christian philosophy of which they gave a rich and exciting vision, by first introducing me to In the Twilight of Western Thought.

James K.A. Smith

Introduction by R.J. Rushdoony

(Re-printed from the 1960 and 1968 editions of this book.)

The lectures in this book are Dooyeweerd's own introduction to his philosophy and an excellent guide to the study of his recently translated A New Critique of Theoretical Thought (4 vols.).[1] Again, J. M. Spier's two studies, What is Calvinistic Philosophy?,[2] and especially An Introduction to Christian Philosophy,[3] provide a valuable analysis of Dooyeweerd's thinking. Our purpose therefore will not be a review of his already ably surveyed thought but an analysis of its general significance.

Dooyeweerd would be the first to disclaim originality, or that his is a final system, but rather declares that his is a development of Christian philosophy on the biblical foundations of John Calvin and Abraham Kuyper. As such, his philosophy is of major importance and of far-reaching implications.

Central to Dooyeweerd's position is the insistence that truly Christian philosophy can alone be critical, and that non-Christian philosophy is inevitably dogmatical. Basic to all non-Christian philosophies are certain far-reaching pre-theoretical commitments or presuppositions which are basically religious. Man assumes the self-sufficiency and autonomy of his philosophical thought. He makes God relative, and his thought, or some aspect of creation, absolute. As a result of this attitude, man, in his pretended autonomy, immediately finds that, not only is the world of everyday experience a problem, but that he is a problem to himself. Wherever man has, in terms of this presupposition, tried to think philosophically, he has found it all too easy, whether in China or in the West, to end up in skepticism even concerning his own existence, or at least of his thinking processes. As a result, he finds himself often caught between the tension of radical doubt and an acceptance of all perception as substantial because the perceiving subject, man, in his thinking is himself substance, i. e., being that subsists in itself. This is the paradox so ably set forth in Hume in part and clearly in Kant. Substance ceased to be metaphysical for Kant and became epistemological, a form or category of thought. A similar paradox seems to have existed in the philosophy of Metrodorus of Chios, a fourth century B.C. Greek skeptic, who could affirm these two things:

---

1   Presbyterian and Reformed Publishing Co. (Philadelphia).
2   Wm. B. Erdmans Publishing Co. (Grand Rapids).
3   Presbyterian and Reformed Publishing Co. (Philadelphia).

137

"None of us knows anything, not even whether we know or do not know, nor do we know whether not knowing and knowing exist, nor in general whether there is anything or not.
2. Everything exists which anyone perceives."[1]

Here is a hapless Scylla and Charybdis with no middle course. As a result of this dogmatic character of non-Christian philosophy, the naive experience of reality becomes a problem, and the men of philosophy become darker than children in their light. Philosophy must resort to antinomies and paradoxes, because its basically religious faith is apostate faith and hence with no law or norm beyond itself or some aspect of creation. It cannot absolutize any aspect of that created order, which has meaning because created and sustained by God, without obscuring or destroying meaning, and also creating insoluble tensions in that order. Dooyeweerd has in particular analyzed the hapless tensions of Hellenic, medieval, and humanist cultures, as against the presuppositions of truly Christian culture, the fundamental motives of cultures being in essence religious and a product of the basic pre-theoretical commitments of man. The tensions of each culture are regarded as basic tensions of life itself by the members of that culture, because they assume to be ultimate that which is actually a religious condition and ground of their own thought. Each culture, however, is a product of its philosophy, and its philosophy is the expression of its religious presuppositions. The philosophy and the religious presuppositions may change in form, but basic to all non-Christian cultures is the dogma of the autonomy of theoretical thought and its ostensibly critical and non-religious character. It is this dogma which Dooyeweerd so thoroughly challenges and exposes, while delineating the framework of Christian philosophy and culture. In doing this, he is, as Cornelius Van Til has pointed out, "as unashamed as was Calvin in his insistence that man's pre-theoretical commitments determine his outlook in philosophy."[2]

Dooyeweerd, together with Vollenhoven, has developed the Philosophy of the Wetsidee, of the Cosmonomic-Idea. It is impossible, Dooyeweerd holds, to argue across systems, because each can "prove" the error of the other in terms of its basic presuppositions. These basic presuppositions are by no means philosophic but are "self-evident" prejudices of a religious nature. These religious dogmas are assumed to be axioms of thought and remain unexamined and undetected because the non-Christian has no vantage from which to be critical of philosophy; he has no Archimedean point within creation. Dooyeweerd, on the other hand, by beginning with the biblical presuppositions, is able, because the cosmos is in all of its aspects ordered by law instituted by the

---

1   Kathleen Freeman: Vanilla to the PreSocratic Philosophies, Harvard, 1957, p.120 f.
2   C. Van Til in The Westminster Theological Journal, May, 1955 XVII, 2, p.182 f.

Creator-Redeemer, to be critical in a way non-Christian philosophy cannot be.

What is the outcome of this approach to philosophy and culture? Non-Christian philosophy and culture by its very nature, tends inevitably to tension, paradox and antinomy. It cannot do justice to naive experience and inevitably emasculates both life and thought. Two examples of this will suffice.

First, let us consider the implications of Joseph Haroutunian's Lust For Power. For Haroutunian, power is a dangerous thing, and man's desire for power is "the prime unreason in human life and bedevils the whole existence of man." It is a product of the "despair of being" and is thus a substitute for life and yet as a condition of life "becomes more valuable than life."

> "No amount of power can change being's being in relation to nonbeing, or remove the dread in human existence. Power rather establishes dread and much power turns it into a panic. This is why the more powerful men are, the more dangerous they are. This is why men of power are exposed to arbitrary and irrational action which lets loose torrents of devastating evil. There is no telling when they will make a 'mistake' which will mean wholesale misery and even death. Great men or men of power are men who are 'at their rope's end.' Power is the last substitute for life which can be proposed in this world."[1]

Power is seen as opposed to and a substitute for love. "A man isolated from his fellowmen seeks mastery over them as the best means of security and contentment. He hopes to do with power what he has failed to do without love." "Love for life is the only authentic antidote to lust in general and to lust for power in particular."[2] It is apparent that Haroutunian sees power only as an evil, and as opposed to love, never as an aspect of the divine image in man. Dooyeweerd, in his second lecture on "The Sense of History," comments, "Even the most terrible misuse of cultural power in our sinful world cannot make power itself sinful, nor can it detract from the normative sense of man's cultural vocation." If a fallen world is the source of norms, then inevitably an emasculating tension results; love is opposed to power, nature to freedom, or nature to grace, matter to form, and so on. To absolutize one aspect of creation is to distort all of creation and render it void of meaning. As modern man attempts to empty God and man of power, he empties love of power and meaning also. Karl Barth declares, "God and 'power in itself' are mutually exclusive. God is the essence of the possible; but 'power in itself' is

---

1   Joseph Haroutunian, Lust for Power, Scribner's, New York, 1949 pp.74-76.
2   Ibid., pp.38, 140.

the essence of the impossible."[1] By making God "the essence of the possible," that is, with unrealized potentialities, he also makes God destructive of every possible norm. Similarly, according to Plutarch, the Temple of Isis at Sais bore this inscription of the deity's statement:

"I am all that has come into being, and that which is, and that which shall be; and no man hath lifted my veil."

In terms of this, God is not an everlasting being but an ever-becoming, non-personal and identifiable with the cosmos and its process. In sharp opposition to this, as John presented the divine norm to the church, he identified God as He "which is, and which was, and which is to come" (Revelation 1:4), that is, as the eternal one who manifests Himself in history, and, as creator, redeemer and judge, "is to come." Only such a God can provide man with a true cultural vocation and a norm whereby he is able to be critical and constructive. The Christian man, faithful to this norm, can do justice to his experience and his vocation, whereas the non-Christian emasculates himself and his world as the necessary consequence of his immanence-standpoint.

Second, let us examine Rudolf Bultmann on science. In his demythologizing, Bultmann openly avows that "the modern world-view" is his criterion. He recognizes that the results of science vary from age to age, but asserts the principles to be permanent, and hence to be man's guide rather than the mythological which he sees in Scripture. Thus, having made science the source of "permanent principles," Bultmann has apparently found a new source of norms, one within the cosmos. Actually, however, having made the relative absolute, he finds it also become demonic. Science now becomes the source of "man-made security." "The scientific world-view engenders a great temptation, namely, that man strive for mastery over the world and over his own life."[2] "Science now becomes the builder of countless towers of Babel which history must destroy, and is the implicit source of the demonic."[3] There follows then the necessity that "In faith I realize that the scientific world-view does not comprehend the whole reality of the world and of human life, but faith does not offer another general world-view which corrects science in its statements on its own level. Rather faith acknowledges that the world-view given by science is a necessary means for doing our work within the world."[4] As a vantage point of defense and perspective against this scientific juggernaut, Bultmann finds "genuine freedom" only in "freedom from the motivation of the moment," that is, history and the cosmos, and this is only possible in "a law which has its

1 Karl Barth: Dogmatics in Outline. 1949, Philosophical Library, New York, p.48.
2 Rudolf Bultmann: Jesus Christ and Mythology, Scribner's 1958, pp.35-39.
3 Ibid., pp.39, 40, 42.
4 Ibid., p.65.

origin and reason in the beyond .... the law of God."[1] And yet, because God cannot act, and the only permanent principles are from science, which is itself now the source of the demonic, security is impossible, and "He who abandons every form of security shall find true security." Demythologizing is equated with justification as the means of salvation, because it destroys every longing for security.[2] Salvation is thus a permanent state of anxiety and neurosis, and the world a profane place.

Here indeed is an emasculation of life, science, history and law. Bultmann begins by deifying science as the source of permanent principles and ends by regarding it as the great temptation to a false security, as the source in effect of the demonic. Dooyeweerd begins by denying that science is the source of permanent principles and ends by establishing scientific activity as a part of man's vocation and calling. In terms of the divine image he bears, man is called to exercise, among other things, knowledge and dominion in the scientific spheres by subduing the earth. Science is an aspect of his divine vocation in a world of law and a legitimate area of holy activity. The view thus which seemingly "rejects" science becomes the only source of true science, whereas any view which makes absolute that which is relative ends up by destroying the value of that aspect of creation and emasculating life and experience. The cultural and historical, as well as philosophical, implications of Dooyeweerd's position are thus far-reaching.[3] Here is a philosophy with universality and power. Its extensive influence already in Europe is thus not to be wondered at.

Two minor points may be noted. Dooyeweerd has been criticized for using the word motive instead of motif. Let us note, however, the difference between these two words. Motive means 1) that which incites to motive or action; e) a predominant idea; design. Motif means the leading feature in literary or artistic work, especially in music. Motif implies a conscious and deliberate pattern. Motive implies exactly what Dooyeweerd is concerned with, the religious presuppositions of a culture, the ground of thought rather than the product of thought, as with motif.

Again, the criticism of certain aspects of Dooyeweerd's philosophy have been used as an excuse to evade the force of the whole. But Dooyeweerd, no more than Calvin and Kuyper before him, has arrived at a final formulation or is free from occasional defects or inconsistencies. These, however, surely need to be noted, but cannot be used as an excuse to evade the main thrust of his philosophy which has not been

---

1   Ibid., p.41.
2   Ibid., p.84.
3   An excellent application of one aspect of this philosophy is to be found in H. Van Riessen: The Society of the Future (Presbyterian and Reformed Publishing Co.).

met or successfully challenged. It gives important and exciting direction to present and future thought and action and is, in the fullest sense of the word, a Christian philosophy and a great one.

Rousas John Rushdoony
Santa Cruz, Calif.

January 1960

Glossary

[The following glossary of Dooyeweerd's technical terms and neologisms is reproduced and edited by Daniël F. M. Strauss, with the permission of its author, Albert M. Wolters, from C. T. McIntire, ed., The Legacy of Herman Dooyeweerd: Reflections on Critical Philosophy in the Christian Tradition (Lanham MD, 1985), pp. 167-171.]

THIS GLOSSARY OF HERMAN DOOYEWEERD'S terms is an adapted version of the one published in L. Kalsbeek, Contours of a Christian Philosophy (Toronto: Wedge, 1975). It does not provide exhaustive technical definitions but gives hints and pointers for a better understanding. Entries marked with an asterisk are those terms which are used by Dooyeweerd in a way which is unusual in English-speaking philosophical contexts and are, therefore, a potential source of misunderstanding. Words or phrases in small caps and beginning with a capital letter refer to other entries in this glossary.

* Analogy (see LAW-SPHERE) – Collective name for a RETROCIPATION or an ANTICIPATION.

* Anticipation – An ANALOGY within one MODALITY referring to a later modality. An example is "efficiency," a meaning-moment which is found within the historical modality, but which points forward to the later economic modality. Contrast with RETROCIPATION.

* Antinomy – Literally "conflict of laws" (from Greek anti, "against," and nomos, "law"). A logical contradiction arising out of a failure to distinguish the different kinds of law valid in different MODALITIES. Since ontic laws do not conflict (Principium Exclusae Antinomiae), an antinomy is always a logical sign of ontological reductionism.

* Antithesis – Used by Dooyeweerd (following Abraham Kuyper) in a specifically religious sense to refer to the fundamental spiritual opposition between the kingdom of God and the kingdom of darkness. See Galatians 5:17. Since this is an opposition between regimes, not realms, it runs through every department of human life and culture, including philosophy and the academic enterprise as a whole, and through the heart of every believer as he or she struggles to live a life of undivided allegiance to God.

143

Aspect – A synonym for MODALITY.

Cosmonomic idea – Dooyeweerd's own English rendering of the Dutch term wetsidee. Occasionally equivalents are "transcendental ground idea" or "transcendental basic idea". The intention of this new term is to bring to expression that there exists an unbreakable coherence between God's law (nomos) and created reality (cosmos) factually subjected to God's law.

Dialectic – In Dooyeweerd's usage: an unresolvable tension, within a system or line of thought, between two logically irreconcilable polar positions. Such a dialectical tension is characteristic of each of the three non-Christian GROUND-MOTIVES which Dooyeweerd sees as having dominated Western thought.

*Enkapsis (enkaptic) – A neologism borrowed by Dooyeweerd from the Swiss biologist Heidenhain, and derived from the Greek enkaptein, "to swallow up." The term refers to the structural interlacements which can exist between things, plants, animals, and societal structures which have their own internal structural principle and independent qualifying function. As such, enkapsis is to be clearly distinguished from the part-whole relation, in which there is a common internal structure and qualifying function.

Factual Side – General designation of whatever is subjected to the LAW-SIDE of creation (see SUBJECT-SIDE).

Founding function – The earliest of the two modalities which characterize certain types of structural wholes. The other is called the GUIDING FUNCTION. For example, the founding function of the family is the biotic modality.

* Gegenstand – A German word for "object," used by Dooyeweerd as a technical term for a modality when abstracted from the coherence of time and opposed to the analytical function in the theoretical attitude of thought, thereby establishing the Gegenstand relation. Gegenstand is therefore the technically precise word for the object of SCIENCE, while "object" itself is reserved for the objects of NAIVE EXPERIENCE.

Ground-motive – The Dutch term grondmotief, used by Dooyeweerd in the sense of fundamental motivation, driving force. He distinguished four basic ground-motives in the history of Western civilization:
(1) form and matter, which dominated pagan Greek philosophy; (2) nature and grace, which underlay medieval Christian synthesis thought (3) nature and freedom, which has shaped the philosophies of modern times; and (4) creation, fall, and redemption, which lies at the root of a radical and integrally scriptural philosophy.

Guiding function – The highest subject function of a structural whole (e.g. stone, animal, business enterprise, or state). Except in the case of humans, this function is also said to QUALIFY the structural whole. It is called the guiding function because it "guides" or "leads" its earlier functions. For example, the guiding function of a plant is the biotic. The physical function of a plant (as studied, e.g. by biochemistry) is different from physical functioning elsewhere because of its being "guided" by the biotic. Also called "leading function".

* Heart – The concentration point of human existence; the supratemporal focus of all human temporal functions; the religious root unity of humans. Dooyeweerd says that it was his rediscovery of the biblical idea of the heart as the central religious depth dimension of human multifaceted life which enabled him to wrestle free from neo-Kantianism and phenomenology. The Scriptures speak of this focal point also as "soul," "spirit," and "inner man." Philiosophical equivalents are Ego, I, I-ness, and Selfhood. It is the heart in this sense which survives death, and it is by the religious redirection of the heart in regeneration that all human temporal functions are renewed.

* Immanence Philosophy – A name for all non-Christian philosophy, which tries to find the ground and integration of reality within the created order. Unlike Christianity, which acknowledges a transcendent Creator above all things, immanence philosophy of necessity absolutizes some feature or aspect of creation itself.

* Individuality-structure – This term represents arguably one of the most difficult concepts in Dooyeweerd's philosophy. Coined in both Dutch and English by Dooyeweerd himself it has led sometimes to serious misunderstandings amongst scholars. Over the years there have been various attempts to come up with an alternate term, some of which are described below, but in the absence of a consensus it was decided to leave the term the way it is.

It is the general name or the characteristic law (order) of concrete things, as given by virtue of creation. Individuality-structures belong to the law-side of reality. Dooyeweerd uses the term individuality-structure to indicate the applicability of a structural order for the existence of individual entities. Thus the structural laws for the state, for marriage, for works of art, for mosquitoes, for sodium chloride, and so forth are called individuality-structures. The idea of an individual whole is determined by an individuality-structure which precedes the theoretical analysis of its modal functions. The identity of an individual whole is a relative unity in a multiplicity of functions. (See MODALITY.) Van Riessen prefers to call this law for entities an identity-structure, since as such it guarantees the persistent identity of all entities (Wijsbegeerte, Kampen 1970, p.158). In his work (Alive, An Enquiry into the Origin and Meaning of Life, 1984, Ross House Books, Vallecito, California), M. Verbrugge introduces his own distinct systematic account concerning the nature of (what he calls) functors, a word first introduced by Hendrik Hart for the dimension of individuality-structures (cf. Hart: Understanding Our World, Towards an Integral Ontology, New York 1984, cf.pp.445-446). As a substitute for the notion of an individuality-structure, Verbrugge advances the term: idionomy (cf. Alive, pp.42, 81ff., 91ff.). Of course this term may also cause misunderstanding if it is taken to mean that each individual creature (subject) has its own unique law. What is intended is that every type of law (nomos) is meant to delimit and determine unique subjects. In other words, however specified the universality of the law may be, it can never, in its bearing upon unique individual creatures, itself become something uniquely individual. Another way of grasping the meaning of Dooyeweerd's notion of an individuality-structure is, in following an oral suggestion by Roy Clouser (Zeist, August 1986), to call it a type-law (from Greek: typonomy). This simply means that all entities of a certain type conform to this law. The following perspective given by M.D. Stafleu elucidates this terminology in a systematic way (Time and Again, A Systematic Analysis of the Foundations of Physics, Wedge Publishing Foundation, Toronto 1980, p.6, 11): typical laws (type-laws / typonomies, such as the Coulomb law – applicable only to charged entities and the Pauli principle – applicable only to fermions) are special laws which apply to a limited class of entities only, whereas modal laws hold universally for all possible entities. D.F.M. Strauss ('Inleiding tot die Kosmologie,' SACUM, Bloemfontein 1980) introduces the expression entity structures. The term entity comprises both the individuality and the identity of the thing concerned – therefore it accounts for the respective emphases found in Dooyeweerd's notion of individuality-structures and in Van Riessen's notion of identity structures. The following words of Dooyeweerd show that both the individuality and identity of an entity is determined by its 'individuality-structure': "In general we can establish that the factual temporal duration of a thing as an individual and identical whole is dependent on the preservation of its structure of individuality" (A New Critique of Theoretical Thought, Vol.III:79).

Irreducibility (irreducible) – Incapability of theoretical reduction. This is the negative way of referring to the unique distinctiveness of things and aspects which we find everywhere in creation and which theoretical thought must respect. Insofar as everything has its own peculiar created nature and character, it cannot be understood in terms of categories foreign to itself.

* Law – The notion of creational law is central to Dooyeweerd's philosophy. Everything in creation is subject to God's law for it, and accordingly law is the boundary between God and creation. Scriptural synonyms for law are "ordinance," "decree," "commandment," "word," and so on. Dooyeweerd stresses that law is not in opposition to but the condition for true freedom. See also NORM and LAW-SIDE.

Law-Side – The created cosmos, for Dooyeweerd, has two correlative "sides": a law-side and a factual side (initially called: SUBJECT-SIDE). The former is simply the coherence of God's laws or ordinances for creation; the latter is the totality of created reality which is subject to those laws. It is important to note that the law-side always holds universally.

Law-Sphere (see MODAL STRUCTURE and MODALITY) – The circle of laws qualified by a unique, irreducible and indefinable meaning-nucleus is known as a law-sphere. Within every law-sphere temporal reality has a modal function and in this function is subjected (French: sujet) to the laws of the modal spheres. Therefore every law-sphere has a law-side and a sub-ject-side that are given only in unbreakable correlation with each other. (See DIAGRAM on p.151.)

* Meaning – Dooyeweerd uses the word "meaning" in an unusual sense. By it he means the referential, non-self-sufficient character of created reality in that it points beyond itself to God as Origin. Dooyeweerd stresses that real-ity is meaning in this sense and that, therefore, it does not have meaning. "Meaning" is the Christian alternative to the metaphysical substance of im-manence philosphy. "Meaning" becomes almost a synonym for "reality." Note the many compounds formed from it: meaning-nucleus, meaning-side, meaning-moment, meaning-fullness.

* Meaning-nucleus – The indefinable core meaning of a MODALITY.

Modality (See MODAL STRUCTURE and LAW-SPHERE) – One of the fifteen fundamental ways of being distinguished by Dooyeweerd. As modes of be-ing, they are sharply distinguished from the concrete things which function within them. Initially Dooyeweerd distinguished fourteen aspects only, but since 1950 he introduced the kinematical aspect of uniform movement be-tween the spatial and the physical aspects. Modalities are also known as "modal functions," "modal aspects," or as "facets" of created reality. (See DIAGRAM on p.151.)

Modal Structure (see MODALITY and LAW-SPHERE) – The peculiar constella-tion, in any given modality, of its meaning-moments (anticipatory, retrocipatory, nuclear). Contrast INDIVIDUALITY-STRUCTURE.

* Naive experience – Human experience insofar as it is not "theoretical" in Dooyeweerd's precise sense."Naive" does not mean unsophisticated. Some-times called "ordinary" or "everyday" experience. Dooyeweerd takes pains to emphasize that theory is embedded in this everyday experience and must not violate it.

Norm (normative) – Postpsychical laws, that is, modal laws for the analytical through pistical law-spheres (see LAW-SPHERE and DIAGRAM on p.151). These laws are norms because they need to be positivized (see POSITIVIZE) and can be violated, in distinction from the "natural laws" of the pre-analytical spheres which are obeyed involuntarily (e.g., in a digestive process).

* Nuclear-moment – A synonym for MEANING-NUCLEUS and LAW-SPHERE, used to designate the indefinable core meaning of a MODALITY or aspect of created reality.

* Object – Something qualified by an object function and thus correlated to a subject function. A work of art, for instance, is qualified by its correlation to the human subjective function of aesthetic appreciation. Similarly, the elements of a sacrament are pistical objects.

Opening process – The process by which latent modal anticipations are "opened" or actualized. The modal meaning is then said to be "deepened." It is this process which makes possible the cultural development (differentiation) of society from a primitive ("closed," undifferentiated) stage. For example, by the opening or disclosure of the ethical anticipation in the juridical aspect, the modal meaning of the legal aspect is deepened and society can move from the principle of "an eye for an eye" to the consideration of extenuating circumstances in the administration of justice.

* Philosophy – In Dooyeweerd's precise systematic terminology, philosophy is the encyclopedic science, that is, its proper task is the theoretical investigation of the overall systematic integration of the various scientific disciplines and their fields of inquiry. Dooyeweerd also uses the term in a more inclusive sense, especially when he points out that all philosophy is rooted in a pretheoretical religious commitment and that some philosophical conception, in turn, lies at the root of all scientific scholarship.

Positivize – A word coined to translate the Dutch word positiveren, which means to make positive in the sense of being actually valid in a given time or place. For example, positive law is the legislation which is in force in a given country at a particular time; it is contrasted with the legal principles which lawmakers must positivize as legislation. In a general sense, it refers to the responsible implementation of all normative principles in human life as embodied, for example, in state legislation, economic policy, ethical guidelines, and so on.

Qualify – The GUIDING FUNCTION of a thing is said to qualify it in the sense of characterizing it. In this sense a plant is said to be qualified by the biotic and a state by the juridical [aspects].

* Radical – Dooyeweerd frequently uses this term with an implicit reference to the Greek meaning of radix = root. This usage must not be confused with the political connotation of the term radical in English. In other works Dooyeweerd sometimes paraphrases his use of the term radical with the phrase: penetrating to the root of created reality.

* Religion (religious) – For Dooyeweerd, religion is not an area or sphere of life but the all-encompassing and direction-giving root of it. It is service of God (or a substitute no-god) in every domain of human endeavor. As such, it is to be sharply distinguished from religious faith, which is but one of the many acts and attitudes of human existence. Religion is an affair of the HEART and so directs all human functions. Dooyeweerd says religion is "the innate impulse of the human selfhood to direct itself toward the true or

toward a pretended absolute Origin of all temporal diversity of meaning" (A New Critique of Theoretical Thought, Vol.I, 1953, p.57).

* Retrocipation – A feature in one MODALITY which refers to, is reminiscent of, an earlier one, yet retaining the modal qualification of the aspect in which it is found. The "extension" of a concept, for example, is a kind of logical space: it is a strictly logical affair, and yet it harks back to the spatial modality in its original sense. See ANTICIPATION.

* Science – Two things are noted about Dooyeweerd's use of the term "science". In the first place, as a translation of the Dutch word wetenschap (analogous to the German word Wissenschaft), it embraces all scholarly study – not only the natural sciences but also the social sciences and the humanities, including theology and philosophy. In the second place, science is always, strictly speaking, a matter of modal abstraction, that is, of analytically lifting an aspect out of the temporal coherence in which it is found and examining it in the Gegenstand relation. But in this investigation it does not focus its theoretical attention upon the modal structure of such an aspect itself; rather, it focuses on the coherence of the actual phenomena which function within that structure. Modal abstraction as such must be distinguished from NAIVE EXPERIENCE. In the first sense, therefore, "science" has a wider application in Dooyeweerd than is usual in English-speaking countries, but in the second sense it has a more restricted, technical meaning.

Sphere Sovereignty – A translation of Kuyper's phrase souvereiniteit in eigen kring, by which he meant that the various distinct spheres of human authority (such as family, church, school, and business enterprise) each have their own responsibility and decision-making power which may not be usurped by those in authority in another sphere, for example, the state. Dooyeweerd retains this usage but also extends it to mean the IRREDUCIBILITY of the modal aspects. This is the ontical principle on which the societal principle is based since each of the societal "spheres" mentioned is qualified by a different irreducible modality.

* Subject – Used in two senses by Dooyeweerd: (1) "subject" as distinguished from LAW, (2) "subject" as distinguished from OBJECT. The latter sense is roughly equivalent to common usage; the former is unusual and ambiguous. Since all things are "subject" to LAW, objects are also subjects in the first sense. Dooyeweerd's matured conception, however, does not show this ambiguity. By distinguishing between the law-side and the factual side of creation, both subject and object (sense (2)) are part of the factual side.

Subject-Side – The correlate of LAW-SIDE, preferably called the factual side. Another feature of the factual subject-side is that it is only here that individuality is found.

Substratum – The aggregate of modalities preceding a given aspect in the modal order. The arithmetic, spatial, kinematic, and physical, for example, together form the substratum for the biotic. They are also the necessary foundation upon which the biotic rests, and without which it cannot exist. See SUPERSTRATUM (and the DIAGRAM on p.151).

Superstratum – The aggregate of modalities following a given aspect in the modal order. For example, the pistical, ethical, juridical and aesthetic together constitute the superstratum of the economic. See SUBSTRATUM.

* Synthesis – The combination, in a single philosophical conception, of characteristic themes from both pagan philosophy and biblical religion. It is this feature of the Christian intellectual tradition, present since patristic times, with which Dooyeweerd wants to make a radical break. Epistemologically seen the term synthesis is used to designate the way in which a multiplicity of features is integrated within the unity of a concept. The re-union of the logical aspect of the theoretical act of thought with its non-logical 'Gegenstand' is called an inter-modal meaning-synthesis.

* Time – In Dooyeweerd, a general ontological principle of intermodal continuity, with far wider application than our common notion of time, which is equated by him with the physical manifestation of this general cosmic time. It is, therefore, not coordinate with space. All created things, except the human HEART, are in time. At the law-side time expresses itself as time-order and at the factual side (including subject-subject and subject-object relations) as time duration.

Transcendental – A technical term from the philosophy of Kant denoting the a priori structural conditions which make human experience (specifically human knowledge and theoretical thought) possible. As such it is to be sharply distinguished from the term "transcendent." Furthermore, the basic (transcendental) Idea of a philosophy pre-supposes the transcendent and central sphere of consciousness (the human HEART). This constitutes the second meaning in which Dooyeweerd uses the term transcendental: through its transcendental ground-Idea philosophy points beyond itself to its ultimate religious foundation transcending the realm of thought.

CREATURES SUBJECTED TO CREATIONAL LAWS

Aspects, Entities and Societal Institutions

Law-Spheres (Aspects)		Meaning-nuclei
Certitudinal ▲		certainty (to be sure)
Ethical ▲	Family — Church	love/troth
Juridical ▲	State	retribution
Aesthetical		beautiful harmony
Economical ▲		frugality/avoid excesses
Social	Business	social intercourse
Sign-mode		symbolical signification
Cultural-historical ▾		formative power/control
Logical		analysis
Sensitive-psychical	ANIMALS	sensitivity/feeling
Biotical	PLANTS	organic life
Physical	THINGS	energy-operation
Kinematic		Uniform motion/constancy
Spatial		Continuous extension
Numerical		discrete quantity

Left vertical labels: HUMAN BEINGS — SOCIAL LIFE-FORMS & CULTURAL THINGS

▾ Foundational function of church, state and business   ▲ Qualifying function

Index

154

the human ego 25
theoretical antithesis 10-11, 15-16, 18
theoretical attitude of thought 3, 5-8,
    10-12, 14-15, 27-28, 31, 37, 39, 87,
    91, 99, 107, 113
theoretical axiom 4
theoretical synthesis 14-18, 28, 40
theories of knowledge 14
thing-in-itself 11
Thomson 83
Toynbee 46
traditional theological view of man
    127, 129
transcendence vi, 37, 93, 121, 123
transcendent critique 6
transcendental basic idea 36-37, 40
transcendental basic Ideas 41
transcendental critique 6, 10-11, 17,
    26-27, 33, 36-38, 41, 98, 100
transcendental method 16
transcendental philosophy 6, 16
tribe 72

U

The unfolding process 67

unbreakable coherence 9, 14-15, 65-
    66, 75, 88-89, 104
University of Leyden 110

V

Vatican II 97
Vico 46, 62
Vienna Circle 5

W

the Word-revelation 47, 80, 83, 86,
    97-99, 109, 126-128, 132
Wesselius 119
Western civilization 27, 54-56, 60,
    69, 75, 119-122
Western metaphysics 79
West-Friesland 109
Wines 61
Wolters v, vii, 21, 50
Word of God 30, 42, 45, 82-83, 86,
    90, 95-96, 98-99, 128, 130-132

Z

Zohn 56, 70

CPSIA information can be obtained at www.ICGtesting.com
Printed in the USA
BVOW04s1357110916

461667BV00003B/244/P